Christian
Metaphysics
and
Neoplatonism

Other works of Interest from St. Augustine's Press

Peter Kreeft, *Socrates' Children* (in four volumes):
Ancient, Medieval, Modern, and *Contemporary*

Peter Kreeft, *Summa Philosophica*

Peter Kreeft, *Socratic Logic*

Gerhart Niemeyer, *The Loss and Recovery of Truth*

Stanley Rosen, *Essays in Philosophy* (in two volumes):
Ancient and *Modern*

Stanley Rosen, *Platonic Productions:
Theme and Variations: The Gilson Lectures*

Gabriel Marcel, *The Mystery of Being* (in two volumes):
I: *Reflections and Mystery* and II: *Faith and Reality*

Seth Benardete, *The Archaeology of the Soul:
Platonic Readings for Ancient Poetry and Philosophy*

Philippe Bénéton, *The Kingdom Suffereth Violence:
The Machiavelli / Erasmus / More Correspondence
and other Unpublished Documents*

Rémi Brague, *On the God of the Christians:
(and on one or two others)*

Rémi Brague, *Eccentric Culture: A Theory of Western Citilization*

Pierre Manent, *Seeing Things Politically:
Interviews with Benedicte Delorme-Montini*

Roger Pouivet, *After Wittgenstein, St. Thomas*

Christopher Bruell, *Aristotle as Teacher:
His Introduction to a Philosophic Science*

Richard A. Watson, *Solipsism:
The Ultimate Empiral Theory of Human Existence*

Emanuela Scribano, *A Reading Guide to Descartes'*
Meditations on First Philosophy

Roger Scruton, *The Meaning of Conservatism*

René Girard, *A Theory of Envy: William Shakespeare*

H.D. Gerdil, *The Anti-Emile:
Reflections on the Theory and Practice of Education against the
Principles of Rousseau*

Joseph Cropsey, *On Humanity's Intensive Introspection*

Christian
Metaphysics
and
Neoplatonism

by Albert Camus

Epilogue by
Rémi Brague

Translated with a Preface
and introduction by
Ronald D. Srigley

ST. AUGUSTINE'S PRESS
South Bend, Indiana
in cooperation with
The Eric Voegelin Society

Manufactured in the United States of America

1 2 3 4 5 6   21 20 19 18 17 16 15

Library of Congress Cataloging in Publication Data

Camus, Albert, 1913–1960.
    [Metaphysique chretienne et neoplatonisme. English]
    Christian metaphysics and Neoplatonism : / Albert Camus; translated with
        an Introduction and new preface by Ronald D. Srigley; foreword by Ellis
        Sandoz.
        pages cm
    "In association with the Eric Voegelin Society."
    Includes bibliographical references and index.
    ISBN 978-1-58731-114-7 (hardcover : alk. paper) 1. Christianity –
    Philosophy. 2. Metaphysics. 3. Neoplatonism. 4. Evangelicalism.
    5. Gnosticism. 6. Mysticism. 7. Augustine, Saint, Bishop of Hippo.
    I. Title.
    BR100.C34313 2014
    C190 – dc23   2014009448

St. Augustine's Press
www.staugustine.net

For Kate

Contents

Christian Metaphysics and Neoplatonism

Acknowledgments

I would like to thank my friend Bruce Ward, who first suggested this project to me several years ago. My translation is the fruit of his suggestion, and the latest installment in our ongoing (I will not say eternal) debate about the ancients and the moderns. Tracey Higgin's careful reading of an earlier draft of this manuscript helped me refine my translation significantly and to appreciate the beauty and subtlety of the French language. Dr. Gérard Vallée of McMaster University was a great help in tracking down some of Camus' more obscure ancient terms. He also taught me a thing or two about the nature of the translator's art. Many thanks to my colleague at Laurentian University, Guy Chamberland, who gave generously of his time and talents in tracking down and translating several of Camus' original Latin sources. Thanks go to Beverly Jarrett, director and editor-in-chief of the University of Missouri Press, whose support of my work has been constant and untiring. Thanks also go to Sara Davis and Julie Schorfheide for getting the manuscript into shape. Many thanks also to Mme. Catherine Camus for her encouragement of this project and her permission to reproduce *Métaphysique chrétienne et néoplatonisme* in English translation. Jerry Day has discussed with me or read nearly everything I have thought or written about Camus over the years. His good sense and his friendship are things that have counted for me. From Zdravko Planinc I learned how to read Camus. Thanks to him for a pedagogy that always left room for a second sailing and that wisely kept the important parts of the map blank. A very heartfelt thanks to Susan Srigley for her fine conversation, her constant encouragement, and for her gracious efforts to keep me in the game. Thanks also go to my mother, Joyce Srigley, for her support and for not quitting, even when the chips were down.

A special thanks to the boys, William and Elliott, who never cease to remind me that reading Camus in French is not much without summer basketball and evening swims at cheap-laugh rock. I reserve my deepest thanks for my partner, Kate Tilleczek. Her intelligent and thoughtful reading of this manuscript improved it immeasurably and gently encouraged me to see and describe things as they are—in life as in work. From subtropical coastal plains to the dizzying heights of the Athabasca Pass, I have seen with her rare and distant things, both high and low, and learned life's most beautiful and enduring lessons.

Preface to the St. Augustine's Edition of
Christian Metaphysics and Neoplatism

———————————————————— ⇥⊹

Christian Metaphysics and Neoplatonism examines the transition in the West from classical Greek civilization to Christianity. It is Camus' most extended discussion of the period and his first attempt to explain the novelty of the Christian religion in comparison to the religion and philosophy of the ancients, a subject that would occupy him for the remainder of his career. His argument is essentially Nietzsche's in *The Birth of Tragedy*, though with reservations. Christianity reintroduces into the West the tragic seriousness of the ancient Greeks and thus serves as a corrective to the "womanish flight from seriousness and terror" introduced by Socrates' rationalism, Attic comedy, and Euripides' drama.[1] Like Nietzsche, Camus praises Christianity's achievement while remaining skeptical about its claim to have initiated an unprecedented change in or revelation of our relationship to the divine. Christianity's profound truth lies not in this assertion but in its unacknowledged return to the ancients.

Camus had reservations about the argument. Despite his notion of a Hellenized Christianity and his highly approbative account of Christianity's political importance (it remains "the only effective shield against the calamity of the Western world," he tells us), at the conclusion of *Christian Metaphysics*, he wonders whether he has captured the "profound novelty" of the religion. "But we are also aware that, were it

1. Friedrich Nietzsche, *"The Birth of Tragedy" and "The Case against Wagner,"* trans. Walter Kaufmann (New York: Vintage Books, 1967), 11.

xi

dismantled entirely into foreign elements, we would still recognize it as original because of a more subdued resonance than the world has yet heard." Christianity may have borrowed extensively from the classical traditions of the Eastern Mediterranean basin in order to articulate its central doctrines; and it may have employed Greek formulas in particular to clarify its emotional aspirations; yet despite this "agreement" with the thinking of ancients, there was something in the Christian teaching to which figures such as Plotinus, Celsus, and Porphyry simply could not assent, and with them the entire ancient world.

Camus' explanation of Christianity's novelty in *Christian Metaphysics* is complex and nuanced. However, there is one feature of that explanation that runs throughout the analysis and forms the center around which the other features cluster. This is Christianity's notion of an apocalyptic history and a final redemption in the afterlife. Camus sets aside more common explanations of Christian novelty, such as faith, because faith, with its subordination of reason, is a subsidiary phenomenon devised only to shelter Christianity's primary ambitions from unfettered critical appraisal. These primary ambitions are the real source of its novelty and the true object of Camus' analysis.

Camus' assessment of Christian redemption in *Christian Metaphysics* is mixed. Sometimes he argues that Christianity's apocalypticism is a faithful articulation of its tragic sensibility. Christianity's profound attachment to life (an essential condition of tragedy) is best measured by the imperiousness of its demand that life be continued. Unlike Pascal, who teaches us that being unable to cure death it is best we do not think about it, Camus claims that "[t]he whole effort of Christianity is to oppose itself to this slowness of heart." However, Camus also argues that Christian redemption entails the abandonment of the classical pursuit of the good in favor of a salvation in which nature is escaped rather than perfected. In this reading, the motivation of Christian apocalypticism is not attachment but fear, a fear that is willing to forego attachment in favor of self-interest and is therefore anything but tragic. In a notebook entry from 1940, some three years after the completion of *Christian Metaphysics*, Camus chooses between these interpretations and thus sets the groundwork for his mature assessment of the tradition: "If we tear out the last pages of the New Testament, then what we see set forth is a religion of loneliness and human grandeur. Certainly, its bitterness makes it unbearable. But that is its truth, and the all the rest is a lie."[2]

* * *

Camus never retracted his criticism of the apocalyptic aspirations of the Christian religion. That criticism later became central to *The Myth of Sisyphus* and *The Rebel*, as well as to novels like *The Stranger* and *The Plague*. However, it did not entail for Camus the further denial of God or the sacred. The climate of opinion in which Camus was working was largely unamenable to this type of argument. Christians and their critics alike tended to identify the notion of divinity with the affirmation of an afterlife. In order to articulate his more nuanced account, Camus referred increasingly to paradoxical formulations of the following type: "Secret of my universe: imagine God without the immortality of the soul." "The Greeks made allowances for the divine. But *the divine was not everything*." "I often read that I am atheistic; I hear people speak of my atheism. Yet these words say nothing to me; for me they have no meaning. I do not believe in God and I am not an atheist."[3]

There are a number of important things being said here, all of which require interpretation. Although the Christian account retained the notion of a "spiritual nature" and therefore offered some ground of resistance to the violence of the age, there was for Camus something about its notion of divinity and its apocalyptic ambitions that not only proved ineffective in resisting that violence, but may also have abetted it, however unwittingly. There are several ways in which Camus makes the argument, some of which are familiar to scholars. One of the more powerful is his claim that Christianity's emphasis on transcendence as the most important index of divinity and redemption contributed in a decisive way to emptying the world of its substance.[4] There is nothing wrong with transcendence per se. As early as *The Myth of Sisyphus*

2. Albert Camus, *Notebooks 1935–1942*, trans. Philip Thody (New York: Paragon House, 1991), 174. The same assessment is offered in *The Fall*, only from the side of the tradition: "'Why hast thou forsaken me?' – it was a seditious cry, wasn't it? Well, then, the scissors!" Albert Camus, *The Fall*, trans. Justin O'Brien (New York: Vintage International, 1991), 113.

3. Albert Camus, *Notebooks 1942–1951*, trans. Justin O'Brien (New York: Paragon House, 1991), 12. Ibid., 128 (italics in original). Albert Camus, *Notebooks, 1951–1959*, trans. Ryan Bloom (Chicago: Ivan R. Dee, 2008), 112.

4. Albert Camus, *The Rebel*, trans. Anthony Bower (New York: Vintage International, 1991), 190.

Camus had argued that the existential confrontation he aimed to describe was with a "reality that transcends [him] (*une réalité qui le dépasse*)" in various ways.[5] Rather what concerned him was the narrowing and elevating of the term to such a degree that it had the reverse effect of siphoning from the world virtually every last trace of its mystery and meaning. That is why in *The Rebel* Camus agrees with Nietzsche's "paradoxical but significant conclusion that God has been killed by Christianity, in that Christianity has secularized the sacred."[6] The rational, systematic murder of human beings would soon follow this murder of the sacred and holy.

In his 1958 Preface to *The Wrong Side and the Right Side*, Camus wrote, "I wanted to change lives, yes, but not the world which I worshipped as divine."[7] For Camus the mystery or sacred is not an occasional experience of transcendence but something that exists in everything we experience in an essential way. His best art, for instance, lyrical essays like "Return to Tipasa," are extraordinary evocations of that mystery that both enrich our desire and calm our worst fears and fanaticisms. "The secret I am looking for is buried in a valley of olive trees, beneath the grass and cold violets, around an old house that smells of vines."[8] This is not poetic affectation. The secret – the mystery – is *in* such things. There is no adequate name for that mystery. It is not a place, still less an ethic or law. As Camus says earlier in the essay, we live for something that transcends ethics and its nagging complaint against the world. Yet it is present everywhere and to all and the experience of it for Camus provides the wisdom necessary to guide our actions and to teach us that our actions are not everything. By learning to see once again the sacred in everything around us we may find relief from both the elsewhereness of our religious hopes and our modern, willful attempts to realize them.

Christian Metaphysics was the first step of a remarkable intellectual adventure that would lead Camus to redefine and reinvigorate a sense of the sacred for an entire generation.

---

5. Albert Camus, *The Myth of Sisyphus*, trans. Justin O'Brien (London: Penguin Books, 1988), 54; Albert Camus, *Essais* (Paris: Éditions Gallimard, 1965), 139.

6. Albert Camus, *The Rebel*, 69.

7. Albert Camus, *Lyrical and Critical Essays*, trans. Philip Thody & Ellen Conroy Kennedy (New York: Vintage Books, 1970), 7.

8. Ibid., 171.

Christian
Metaphysics
and
Neoplatonism

Translator's Introduction

    In the fall of 1947, Albert Camus wrote in his *Notebooks:* "If, to outgrow nihilism, one must return to Christianity, one may well follow the impulse and outgrow Christianity in Hellenism."[1] A few years later, Camus restated the matter more forcefully and in a way that cleared up any lingering ambiguity about where the line should be drawn between the ancients and the moderns: "Go back to the passage from Hellenism to Christianity, the true and only turning point in history."[2] Camus acknowledges a difference between Christianity and modernity at the same time that he implicates Christianity in the modern project. He also makes it clear that for him the Greeks are the only genuine alternative in the West. They alone possess an account that is free of the limitations of both traditions. These bold claims indicate a direction in Camus' thought that was first articulated and explored in *Christian Metaphysics and Neoplatonism.* His proposed return to its subject matter alone is good evidence of its importance to his central philosophical project. Camus once said of Melville that he only ever wrote one book.[3] I think the same can be said of Camus. At the heart of the mystery out of which that book was written and rewritten are the

---

1. Albert Camus, *Notebooks 1942–1951,* trans. Justin O'Brien (New York: Paragon House, 1991), 183.
2. Ibid., 267.
3. Albert Camus, "Herman Melville," in *Lyrical and Critical Essays,* ed. Philip Thody, trans. Ellen Conroy Kennedy (New York: Knopf, 1968), 291. "But it seems to me (and this would deserve detailed development) that Melville never wrote anything but the same book, which he began again and again."

fundamental questions about human life that he first explored in *Christian Metaphysics.*

Camus wrote *Christian Metaphysics* in order to fulfil the thesis requirement for his *diplôme d'études supérieures* at the University of Algiers. A brief history of Camus' education and his life at this time will help situate the text for contemporary readers.

In June of 1932, at the age of nineteen, Camus received his *baccalauréat* from the Grand Lycée.[4] This is the European equivalent of a high school diploma. Jean Grenier, his principal instructor at the lycée, became an important intellectual influence on Camus in the early stages of his career and remained a close friend in later years. In mainland France, students who wished to pursue university degrees were required to complete two preparatory years of study before entering their programs. These were called the *hypokhâgne* and *khâgne* years, respectively. In Paris, completion of these years would normally lead to acceptance into the prestigious École Normale Supérieure and subsequently to a teaching position. The full range of such academic programs were not offered in the French colonies, however. In the case of Camus' native Algeria, only the *hypokhâgne* year was available. Camus successfully completed his in 1933 and began his studies at the University of Algiers in the fall of the same year.

The program at the University of Algiers lasted three years and comprised two parts. Completion of the first two years of the program led to the *licence de philosophie.* Students were required to complete four *certificats* in different areas of specialization. The content of these areas was completely open. Each professor would select his own materials, and classes were small and operated more like advanced seminars than undergraduate lectures, with students making oral presentations followed by open discussions. Each *certificat* would culminate in a final examination. Camus' chosen areas of specialization were as follows: *certificat de morale et sociologie, certificat de psychologie, certificat des études littéraires classiques,* and *certificat de logique et philosophie générale.* Camus successfully completed all his *certificats* by June 1935, well within the two-year limit specified by the program.

---

4. The following biographical remarks are gathered largely from Herbert R. Lottman's and Oliver Todd's excellent biographies of Camus. Herbert R. Lottman, *Albert Camus: A Biography* (New York: George Braziller, 1981), 38–76. Oliver Todd, *Albert Camus: A Life,* trans. Benjamin Ivry (New York: Alfred A. Knopf, 1997).

The third year of the program was taken up with the writing of a dissertation. Students who successfully completed this requirement received the *diplôme d'études supérieures,* which made them eligible to take the examinations for the *agrégation.* This important examination was the path to a teaching career in France or abroad, or to doctoral studies.[5] Herbert Lottman claims that only a third of the students enrolled in the program managed to complete their *diplôme,* so given the circumstances it was no small achievement on Camus's part. In North American terms, the *diplôme* is roughly the equivalent of a master's degree.

Indications are that Camus fully intended to sit the examinations for the *agrégation* and to pursue a career in teaching as a means to support himself.[6] He had come from a poor working-class family and so had no illusions about poverty, and he had few if any complexes about the need for money. Despite the occasional assistance he received from his uncle's family and his mother-in-law, he was always compelled by circumstances to work in order to support himself.[7] This continued over the course of his studies, and there is no reason to think that Camus ever imagined it would be otherwise. We always tend to think of writers as having emerged full-blown into the world and with knowledge comparable to our own about their future accomplishments. But at this stage in his life, Camus was not yet Camus. He was, instead, a young writer with a remarkable talent who fully expected to work to support himself and who worried that these necessities might interfere with his literary projects. Teaching likely seemed a good bet to him; and if he had any doubts, he had the example of his mentor, Grenier, to guide him.[8]

5. Lottman, *Camus: A Biography,* 65.

6. Roger Quilliot confirms this ambition in his introduction to the Pléiade edition of *Christian Metaphysics and Neoplatonism,* citing Charles Poncet as his source: "The logical outcome of the *licence de philosophie* is the *diplôme d'études supérieures,* prelude to the application for the *agrégation,* the highest competitive examination for teachers in France. Camus, in 1936, did not despair of achieving it: according to Charles Poncet, he dreamed of a foreign appointment that would leave him sufficient leisure for his personal work." Albert Camus, *Essais* (Paris: Éditions Gallimard, 1965), 1220.

7. Lottman, *Camus: A Biography,* 49, 62.

8. Lottman tells us that Grenier's own literary career really only began after he had moved to Algiers. Prior to that move, his entire published work consisted of a few insignificant essays. However, in 1930, after arriving in Algiers, he published no less than four essays and began to publish a series of small books of philosophy. Ibid., 42.

In the end, Camus' poor health prevented him from sitting the examinations for the *agrégation* and becoming a teacher. In France, a teaching position was a state appointment, and candidates had to pass a physical examination to prove that they were in satisfactory health in order to receive one. Camus had been diagnosed with tuberculosis, and in the mid-twentieth century, tuberculosis was still an incurable disease in Europe. The French government was apparently unwilling to gamble on a man whose chances of survival were limited at best. Camus did what he could to overcome this impediment, as he would a few years later with regard to military service, but to no avail.[9] As Lottman writes, "Camus would later tell Jean Grenier that a special commission of the Government General had deliberated at length on his case, finally issuing a definitive refusal of the medical certificate required for the *agrégation*. According to Jacques Heurgon, Camus's request for a medical certificate was twice rejected."[10]

René Poirier supervised Camus' graduate studies and the writing of *Christian Metaphysics*. He was assisted by Grenier, who was also appointed to the university. Poirier had taught at a lycée in Chartres and at the University of Montpellier before being transferred to Algeria. He was disliked by many of the students because he was unsympathetic to their left-leaning politics. Though he was a member of the Communist Party at the time, Camus did not appear to have any trouble with him and sought to avoid unnecessary conflict. Roger Quilliot claims that although Poirier was Camus' supervisor, Grenier was likely the principal influence on his choice of subject for the dissertation.[11] From what we know of Poirier, that subject—the relationship between Hellenism and Christianity, particularly as it is manifest in the works of Plotinus and Augustine—was quite distant from his primary interests, which concerned the philosophy of science.[12] We know, however, that Grenier was encouraging Camus to read modern authors like Kierkegaard, Chestov, and Berdiaev, whose books explored that relationship in a contemporary context.[13] This lends credence to Quilliot's suggestion.

9. Ibid., 208–9.

10. Ibid., 110 n4.

11. Camus, *Essais,* 1220.

12. Todd, *Camus: A Life,* 27.

13. Todd claims that Grenier wanted Camus to write a thesis on the Hindu religion. He also says that Camus chose Plotinus as one of his principal subjects precisely because neither Grenier nor Poirier were experts in the field. Ibid., 43.

Apart from his teachers, perhaps the most important influence on Camus' thinking at this time was Nietzsche; his name appears frequently in Camus' early *Notebooks*. In 1932, Camus published "Essay on Music," which employs Nietzsche's work as a template for the analysis.[14] And in *Christian Metaphysics* itself, *The Birth of Tragedy* is a constant reference point for Camus' attempts to describe the Greeks and to explain how the Christians departed from their teachings. Perhaps the most important aspect of Camus' reading of Nietzsche was his insight into how basic the quarrel between the ancients and the moderns was to his project and the extent to which Nietzsche had sided with the former—and this in opposition to much contemporary scholarship that insisted, and still insists, on identifying Nietzsche with the moderns.[15] Working out the consequences of this insight would be a central feature of all Camus' subsequent books.

In its final form, *Christian Metaphysics* comprises four chapters, each one exploring a different stage or moment in the evolution of Christianity. I discuss the central argument of the text below. Here I offer only a summary of its chapters and their themes. The first chapter, "Evangelical Christianity," examines biblical texts, the critiques of Porphyry and Celsus, and the works of several early church fathers—for example, Clement, Justin, Ignatius, Tertullian—in order to determine the novelty of Christianity in relation to the religious and philosophical thinking of the ancient world. In the second chapter, "Gnosis," Camus argues that Gnosticism was not an exclusively Christian phenomenon but rather a collaborative effort on the part of a diverse group of writers who wanted to reconcile the Greek notion of reason with the emotional aspirations of Christianity toward fulfillment or salvation.[16] Chapter three, "Mystic Reason," is devoted entirely to an analysis of Plotinus's *Enneads*. What Camus discovers in the *Enneads* is an attempt at reconciliation similar to the one found in Gnosticism. However, in the case of

14. Albert Camus, "Essay on Music," in *Youthful Writings*, trans. Ellen Conroy Kennedy (New York: Alfred A. Knopf, 1976), 130–55.

15. A good contemporary example of this type of interpretation can be found in Alexander Nehamas, *Nietzsche: Life as Literature* (Cambridge: Harvard University Press, 1985). For a recent interpretation that is much closer to Camus', see Peter Berkowitz, *Nietzsche: The Ethics of an Immoralist* (Cambridge: Harvard University Press, 1995).

16. See my discussion of Camus' analysis in Ronald D. Srigley, "Albert Camus on Philo and Gnosticism," *Studia Philonica Annual*, no. 305, ed. David Runia, 103–6 (Atlanta: Scholars Press, 1995).

Plotinus, that reconciliation concerns, not Greeks and Christians, but two similarly related aspirations inherent in the Greek traditions of late antiquity. The first of these aspirations is a mystical longing for God and a concern with the destiny of the soul that Camus argues had been gaining ground in the Greek world. The second is an abiding need for rationality or coherence and the notion of a permanent and intelligible order on which such coherence rests for its meaning.

The book's final chapter—"Augustine"—is an analysis of Augustine's attempt to synthesize Hellenism and Christianity. Camus' central claim is that Augustine came much closer to accomplishing this synthesis than did the Gnostics, largely because of Augustine's reliance on the preparatory work of Plotinus. Plotinus made Greek reason more amenable to faith through his notion of participation. Augustine could use this "softened" version of reason to make the Christian teachings concerning the Trinity and the Incarnation seem more plausible to the minds of Greeks and Romans alike. The result of Augustine's effort was the creation of a Christian metaphysics, a combination of Greek philosophy and Christian faith that allowed Christianity to escape its parochial Judaic origins and extend its influence into the Mediterranean world. As Camus writes in the concluding chapter of *Christian Metaphysics,* "the miracle is that the two may not be contradictory."[17]

Camus submitted his dissertation for assessment on May 8, 1936. On May 25, he received notice that it had been passed with a grade of 28 out of 40 and that he had been granted his *diplôme d'études supérieures.*[18] The committee that assessed the work was made up of Poirier, Grenier, and the dean of the university, the Greek historian Louis Gernet. Poirier thought the work was a sound piece of writing. However, he also expressed at least a certain reservation about Camus' philosophical abilities. Lottman tells us that in addition to the normal comments and corrections Poirier made on the text, he had also written: "More a writer than a philosopher."[19] This is an argument that Camus would hear frequently during his career. There are moments when he seems to have been tempted to believe it.[20] It was first made publicly by

---

17. Camus, *Essais,* 1306.

18. A photocopy of the certificate appears in Todd, *Camus: A Life.*

19. Lottman, *Camus: A Biography,* 109.

20. In his notebook Camus wrote: "Why I am an artist and not a philosopher? Because I think according to words and not according to ideas." Camus, *Notebooks 1942–1951,* 113.

Jean-Paul Sartre in his early essay on Camus, "An Explication of *The Stranger.*"[21] Unfortunately for Camus, this argument later became something like the orthodox opinion of his work and was often used to dismiss his essays as beautiful but philosophically weak or even sophomoric literary exercises.[22]

One further technical matter about the text. There has been some dispute about the title of the work. Lottman refers to it as *Neoplatonism and Christian Thought*. This is the title given on the certificate issued to Camus for his *diplôme d'études supérieures*.[23] There is also another contender: an extant typescript of the work, formerly in the possession of Mme. Camus but now in the Camus archive, that bears the title, handwritten, of *Hellenism and Christianity: Plotinus and St. Augustine*. In his introduction to the Pleiade edition of Camus' collected works, Quilliot argues that the true title of the text is *Christian Metaphysics and Neoplatonism*. He says that this is confirmed by his own notes of 1954, presumably taken during conversations with Camus, and by the work of M. Viggiani. He argues that further confirmation can be found in the fact that this is the title of the copy of the manuscript held by the university library of the Sorbonne.[24] The documentary evidence, such as it is, seems to suggest that Quilliot is right. In addition to this evidence, we might also add that the title *Christian Metaphysics and Neoplatonism* has the further advantage of more accurately reflecting the actual substance of Camus' argument in the text.

Though there is more than a little criticism in the remark, it demonstrates that Camus, at least for a time, accepted both the distinction and its application. By the time of *The Rebel*, I think he had rejected both.

21. Jean-Paul Sartre, "An Explication of *The Stranger*," in *Literary and Philosophical Essays of Jean-Paul Sartre*, trans. Annette Michelson (New York: Criterion Books, 1955).

22. The argument is made by friends and enemies alike. Sartre makes it yet again in his reply to Camus concerning *The Rebel*, though this time much more polemically. Jean-Paul Sartre, "Réponse à Albert Camus," *Les Temps Modernes* 82 (August 1952): 334–53. Thomas Merton, following Germaine Brée, makes the claim more gently and sympathetically. See Thomas Merton, "Camus: Journals of the Plague Years," *Sewanee Review* (Autumn 1967): 726. Serge Doubrovsky uses a similar distinction between poet and philosopher to clarify the nature of Camus' work and to defend him against critics who charge him with moralizing. Serge Doubrovsky, "The Ethics of Albert Camus," trans. Sondra Mueller and Jean-Marc Vary, in *Camus: A Collection of Critical Essays*, ed. Germaine Brée (New Jersey: Prentice-Hall, 1962), 72.

23. Todd, *Camus: A Life*. Todd's biography includes an image of the original certificate issued to Camus bearing this title.

24. Camus, *Essais*, 1223.

The only English translation of *Christian Metaphysics and Neo-platonism* currently available is that of Joseph McBride. McBride published his translation in 1992 as a chapter of his own book-length study of Camus' philosophy, *Albert Camus: Philosopher and Littérateur.* His principal aim in that book is to explore Camus' notions of absurdity and authenticity in *The Myth of Sisyphus* and *The Stranger,* to assess the influence of Saint Augustine and Nietzsche on these notions, and to argue that *Christian Metaphysics* played an important role in the construction of those works and notions.

I am sympathetic to McBride's ambition, and I agree with him wholeheartedly about the importance of *Christian Metaphysics.* Apart from writers such as Jacques Hardré, Paul Archambault, and I. H. Walker, who have produced a few scattered studies, commentators have been notably silent about this book and its relationship to Camus' mature thought.[25] As I argue below, there is ample evidence in Camus' *oeuvre* to show that the subject of this early essay remained a central feature of his later books and was essential to both his own philosophical project and his critique of modernity. What is less compelling is the substance of McBride's analysis and the character of his translation. I will discuss McBride's commentary first and then turn to an analysis of his translation.

In his introductory discussion of *Christian Metaphysics,* McBride offers a helpful, nonpartisan summary of the book's four chapters and general structure. That summary is similar to the one offered by Jacques Hardré in his essay, "Camus' Thoughts on Christian Metaphysics and Neoplatonism." What McBride does not do is situate the text in the broader context of Camus' published books or explain the nature of its influence on them. This is surprising because one of McBride's main ambitions was precisely to explore that influence in the case of two of Camus' earliest books, *The Myth* and *The Stranger.* What we find instead are several different thematic interpretations of these books, interspersed with lengthy commentaries on related aspects of Nietzsche's

---

25. Jacques Hardré, "Camus' Thoughts on Christian Metaphysics and Neoplatonism," *Studies in Philology* 64 (1967): 97–108; Paul Archambault, *Camus' Hellenic Sources* (Chapel Hill: University of North Carolina Press, 1972); I. H. Walker, "Camus, Plotinus, and 'Patrie': The Remaking of a Myth," *Modern Languages Review* 77 (1982): 829–39.

or Augustine's work, the whole content of which is then said to be somehow related to the analysis offered in *Christian Metaphysics*. As to the substance of that relationship, McBride's thesis consists of the claim, made largely in the book's conclusion and on the basis of a rather impressionistic reading of a few select passages, that an unfilled "desire for totality" or God in the Christian sense is what gave rise to Camus' notion of absurdity and that this desire remained a constant feature of his mature explorations of the human condition.[26]

McBride's manner of interpretation is not new. It gained popularity in the late sixties and early seventies among readers who saw rightly that there was a good deal more to Camus' work than what the standard existentialist interpretation would allow, and who were curious about his ambiguous relationship to Christianity. The essays and books of writers such as André-A Devaux, Jean Onimus, Henri Peyri, William Hamilton, and Thomas Merton are among the best in this regard.[27] Their efforts to read Camus afresh were certainly welcome and in their own way illuminated important aspects of Camus' critique of modernity. Nonetheless, the results of these studies were very mixed and frequently misleading. The attempt to explore the religious side of Camus' thought and to do so sympathetically often ended by confirming the very existentialist interpretation these writers initially sought to

---

26. Joseph McBride, *Albert Camus: Philosopher and Littérateur* (New York: St. Martin's Press, 1992), 175–77. This is essentially Sartre's interpretation of Camus in his "Réponse à Albert Camus." "But since, according to your own terms, injustice is *eternal*—that is to say, since the absence of God is a constant through the changes of history—the immediate relation, which is always begun anew, of the man who demands *to have* a meaning (that is to say, that a meaning be given to him), to this God, who remains eternally silent, itself transcends History. The tension through which man realizes himself—which is, at the same time, an intuitive joy of being—is therefore a veritable conversion that he snatches from everyday 'restlessness' and from 'history' in order to make it coincide finally with his condition. One can go no farther; no progress can find a place in this instantaneous tragedy." Sartre, "Réponse à Albert Camus," 346. The fact that Sartre's piece is highly polemical does not mean that it is wrong, but we should perhaps pause before accepting its argument, particularly because Camus himself did not accept it.

27. André-A Devaux, "Albert Camus: Le christianisme et l'hellenisme," *Nouvelle Revue Luxembourgeoise* (January–April 1970): 11–30; Jean Onimus, *Albert Camus and Christianity*, trans. Emmett Parker (Tuscaloosa: University of Alabama Press, 1970); Henri Peyri, "Camus the Pagan," in *Camus: A Collection of Critical Essays*, ed. Germaine Brée (Englewood Cliffs, NJ: Prentice Hall, 1962); William Hamilton, "The Christian, the Saint, and the Rebel: Albert Camus," in *Forms of Extremity in the Modern Novel*, ed. Nathan A. Scott Jr. (Richmond: John Knox Press, 1965), 55–74; Merton, "Camus: Journals of the Plague Years"; Albert Camus, *The Plague*, with introduction and commentary by Thomas Merton (New York: Seabury Press, 1968).

challenge. I do not think this outcome was idiosyncratic. Like his religious colleagues, Camus sensed keenly the emptiness of modern life. Also like them, he believed that this emptiness had been caused, at least in part, by a narrowing or impoverishment of the full range of human experience, and thus pointed to some greater or transcendent reality. McBride, like Devaux et al., takes this as evidence of a religious longing in Camus comparable to the one we find in Augustine. But since Camus consistently denied that this longing had any comparable Christian fulfillment, McBride claims that he was left with a conception of human life as ultimately meaningless and morally indifferent.[28]

Despite these harsh and surprising conclusions, McBride praises Camus' effort. Camus' world may well be meaningless, but McBride claims that it is the right kind of meaninglessness.[29] What kind is that? The kind that accepts the Christian notions of God and immortality as the only legitimate sources of meaning even though denying that these things exist. Whatever else we might say about such an argument, its effective truth is to guarantee the supremacy of Christianity and to render all possible alternatives to it at best intellectually suspect and at worst positively dishonest.

There is some evidence in Camus' books to support this type of reading. What it amounts to is a variant of the transcendence/immanence argument so common in Dostoevsky's work and in the contemporary debates between Christians and moderns generally.[30] Camus uses the argument in *The Rebel* as a way to organize his historical analysis of the changes in modern revolutionary movements from the eighteenth

---

28. McBride, *Camus: Philosopher and Littératuer*, 175–76.

29. Ibid., 175.

30. Fyodor Dostoevsky, *The Brothers Karamazov*, trans. Constance Garnett, ed. Ralph E. Matlaw (New York: W. W. Norton & Company, 1976). The passage that most clearly illustrates the argument occurs in book six, "A Russian Monk." There Father Zosima makes the following remarks: "God took seeds from different worlds and sowed them on this earth, and His garden grew up and everything came up that could come up, but what grows lives and is alive only through the feeling of its contact with other mysterious worlds. If that feeling grows weak or is destroyed in you, the heavenly growth will die away in you. Then you will be indifferent to life and even grow to hate it" (299–300). As to the debate between Christians and moderns, see P. Travis Kroeker and Bruce K. Ward, *Remembering the End: Dostoevsky as Prophet to Modernity* (Boulder: Westview Press, 2001), particularly the chapter "Prophecy and Poetics," 9–33, for a recent contribution. As to the moderns, I still like Marx's "Contribution to the Critique of Hegel's Philosophy of Right" for its clarity about the matter. Karl Marx, *Early Writings*, ed. and trans. T. B. Bottomore (New York: McGraw Hill, 1963), 43–59.

century to the mid-twentieth century. According to the argument, the movement from Rousseau to Hegel marks a gradual elimination of all vertical transcendence in favor of a philosophy of pure immanence.[31] The most important consequence of this loss of transcendence was a corresponding loss of moral clarity and firmness. Actions are no longer judged good or bad according to their own intrinsic worth but in terms either of pure historical expediency or of the likelihood that they might precipitate a future realm of freedom which itself is not subject to any moral judgment. The argument's appeal lies both in its simplicity and in the fact that it is often the shared self-understanding of the writers and political figures it seeks to explain.

Despite this appeal, I think Camus had serious reservations about the argument. Those reservations are apparent in a close reading of a book like *The Rebel*, which reveals not one but two different accounts of the nature and origin of modernity. These accounts amount to two different histories of the West and two different assessments of the roles played in it by the Greeks, Christians, and moderns.[32] The second of these histories is the antithesis of the first. Rather than relying on the transcendence/immanence argument and its tacit acceptance of the Christian teaching as the true measure in such matters, it asserts that the real historical departure from the morality and culture of the ancient world occurred with the advent of Christianity, and that whatever the Greeks may have meant by notions like transcendence and immanence, it was not what Christians and moderns mean by them.[33] According to this second history, the Christian differentiation of a radically transcendent

31. Albert Camus, *The Rebel*, trans. Anthony Bower (New York: Vintage Books, 1991). "The regicides of the nineteenth century are succeeded by the deicides of the twentieth century, who draw the ultimate conclusions from the logic of rebellion and want to make the earth a kingdom where man is God" (132). A few pages later Camus writes of Hegel: "Hegel's undeniable originality lies in his definitive destruction of all vertical transcendence—particularly the transcendence of principles" (142). The principles Hegel destroyed were those of the French Revolution, which had already destroyed the more robust idea of God as transcendent.

32. See Ronald D. Srigley, "Eric Voegelin's Camus: The Limitations of Greek Myth in *The Rebel*," paper presented at the meeting of the Eric Voegelin Society, the American Political Science Association Annual Meeting, Philadelphia, 2003.

33. Camus develops the following account in *The Rebel*, which is remarkably similar to a formulation he offers in *Christian Metaphysics:* "Metaphysical rebellion presupposes a simplified view of creation—which was inconceivable to the Greeks. To their minds there were not gods on one side and men on the other, but a series of stages leading from one to the other" (28).

divinity did not make real morality or virtue possible, but rather undermined morality's experiential sources and encouraged a doubt about the morality of virtue from which it has not yet recovered.

While it is true that a book characterized by internal contradictions might be interpreted in any number of different ways, I think there is good evidence to suggest that this second history is Camus' best. It recognizably continues the effort, first undertaken in *Christian Metaphysics* and apparent in everything Camus had written since, not merely to contribute to the debate about the nature of modernity but to change its terms of reference. That change challenged orthodox opinion about the matter in two principal ways: it questioned the idea that Christianity and modernity were as antithetical as their respective adherents claimed; and it strove to take the Greeks seriously and at their own word, rather than yielding to the temptation to interpret them historically either as prototypical Christians or failed moderns.

So much for McBride's analysis of *Christian Metaphysics* and its role in the development of Camus' thought. As to the nature of his translation, I have only a few brief comments to make. The most significant difference between McBride's translation and my own concerns their respective degrees of literalness. Beyond basic questions of accuracy, it is a difficult business to know how an author would sound in a language not his own. Some translators measure the fluency of a translation by its readability, others by its ability to retain the beauty of the original text. Both criteria are reasonable as far as they go, but both tend to measure the success of a translation by linguistic standards proper to the language of translation. Though this may seem both obvious and inevitable in the case of any translation, I think a few nuances are possible. Without suggesting any particular philosophical account of languages and their commensurability or incommensurability, I think it is safe to say that people who speak or write in different languages not only think similar thoughts in different words but also think those thoughts differently. Such differences are more circumscribed in the case of languages that have grown out of a common source language and thus share a wide literary, philosophical, and political background, and are far more acute in the case of those that have not. Nonetheless, even in the former case differences exist; and to my mind, a faithful translation will not try to smooth over the bits that jar or seem unfamiliar, but allow them to stand in order to test the reader's patience and stretch his imagination in the hope that some unsuspected corner of the original text might be revealed. Though McBride's translation is certainly fluent by any reasonable standard, I think it is too readable and perhaps too beautiful in English to retain the kind of literalness I have tried to achieve.

There are other important differences between our translations of *Christian Metaphysics*. McBride has made some effort to clarify Camus' sources and the manner in which he uses and misuses texts. He does a particularly good job with certain irregularities in Camus' biblical citations and in tracking down proper references for his French secondary sources. Occasionally he will point out an inconsistency in Camus' scholarship or an instance in which he appears to be using an original language text but is in fact citing a passage in translation from a secondary source. Some of these discoveries are based on Paul Archambault's literary excavations in *Camus' Hellenic Sources*, and they are helpful as far as they go. In my judgment, however, a more critical version of the text is required.

There are three ways in which the current edition tries to meet this requirement. I offer a much more comprehensive examination of Camus' sources. For instance, in addition to the sort of work done by McBride, wherever possible I track down Camus' many unidentified or partially identified sources, clarify others, correct his transcriptions of both Latin and French texts, and offer proper titles and references for them. I also offer a series of translator's notes that chart Camus' use of the ideas and arguments of *Christian Metaphysics* in subsequent essays and books. Those notes are fairly exhaustive and by themselves give the reader a good sense of the manner in which Camus' thinking about the subject developed over the years and of *Christian Metaphysics'* importance for his mature analyses of modernity, Christianity, and the Greeks.

There is one further way in which my translation differs from McBride's and also improves on it, I think. In the course of his analysis, Camus cites dozens of Greek and Latin texts in French translation. McBride's manner of handling these texts is simply to translate Camus' French edition into English. I have approached the matter differently. Whenever Camus cites an ancient primary source, whether in French translation or in the original language, I have substituted a standard English translation in its place. My reason for doing so with passages in original languages is simple: I want to make Camus' book accessible to a wide range of readers, and too much Latin in the body of the text would have been an unnecessary barrier in that regard. McBride too offers English translations of these Latin texts, but he does not offer references for them. In some instances they are the same as those I have used, in others I have been unable to identify his source, whether it be his own translation or another English edition. The latter explanation seems most likely, because had McBride translated the Latin texts himself, he would have discovered and noted Camus' frequent errors in both transcribing passages and referencing them. Be that as it may. I have followed the same procedure in the case of texts in French translation for the sake of scholarly accuracy. An English translation of a French translation of an original Latin text would in some instances give the reader a better sense of what Camus had before him when writing *Christian Metaphysics.* However, it would do so at the price of placing the reader just one step farther removed from the original source.

Whenever I substitute an English translation in either of these manners, I have placed the full French or original language text in a translator's note, along with a reference for the English translation I have used. On the rare occasion when there is a substantial textual difference between the French and English editions, I have identified it in a note. In instances in which I have been unable to find the source of such a passage, or in which no standard English translation exists, I have simply translated the French text into English. This practice is indicated by means of an asterisk following the translator's note.

One final word about the translation itself. Given the importance of not only the subject matter but also the substance of the analysis of *Christian Metaphysics* for Camus' mature thought, it seems to me that a separate critical edition of the book is long overdue. I hope the current volume satisfies the need for such an edition and helps make this important aspect of Camus' thought better known to a wider English-speaking audience.

The importance of antiquity for Camus' books, particularly of Greek philosophy and Christianity, is a subject that has received only limited attention from Camus scholars and critics. Literary analyses usually ignore such matters in favor of more formal questions concerning the construction of Camus' texts, while the more philosophically inclined of Camus' readers have tended to explore the modern and even post-modern orientation of Camus' writings rather than his relationship to the ancients.[34] The scholarship becomes even more scarce when we look for discussions of *Christian Metaphysics* itself. This might be explained in part by the long absence of an English translation of the book. That explanation would make some sense, at least for the English-speaking world; but my guess is that even here the real reason for the neglect has more to do with contemporary cultural patterns and habits of mind than with the availability of texts. At the end of the day, scholars read and analyze the books and ideas they consider important.

The studies of *Christian Metaphysics* currently available are few in number. The most notable among them are those of I. H. Walker, Jacques Hardré, and Paul Archambault. Though all of these writers share an interest in the text, the aim and comprehensiveness of each of their analyses is quite different. Walker's discussion is thematic and explores Camus' Greek sources, most notably Plotinus's *Enneads*. Hardré's paper is essentially a summary of the argument and structure of *Christian Metaphysics* and a recommendation of further research to map the full extent of Camus' use of Greek and Christian sources. Archambault uses *Christian Metaphysics* as part of a larger project to elucidate the nature and extent of Camus' Greek culture. The following is a brief discussion of their works.

In his essay "Camus, Plotinus, and 'Patrie': The Remaking of a Myth," Walker explores Camus' use of Plotinus in early works like "Essay on Music," "Art in Communion," *Christian Metaphysics, The Wrong Side and the Right Side,* and *Nuptials.* Walker argues that in these texts, the earliest of which predates *Christian Metaphysics* by four years, the Plotinian notion of *patrie* or *royaume* and its existential counterpart, *exil,* became essential features of Camus' analysis of the human condition. Camus used them to explain a wide range of phenomena, from the relation between the real and ideal in a work of art, to the compatibility of moral and aesthetic experience, to the character of travel, and,

---

34. Two examples of this type of reading are Jeffery C. Isaac, *Arendt, Camus, and Modern Rebellion* (New Haven: Yale University Press, 1992), and David Sprintzen, *Camus: A Critical Examination* (Philadelphia: Temple University Press, 1988). There are exceptions to this type of reading. Bruce K. Ward explores Camus' critique of Christianity and his Hellenism in his essay "Christianity and the Modern Eclipse of Nature: Two Perspectives," *Journal of the American Academy of Religion* 63, no. 4 (1995): 823–44.

perhaps most important, to the basic human desire for a homeland and the deep existential unease that accompanies the experience of its loss or absence.

In his article, Walker does a good job of tracking down the various ways in which Camus incorporates Plotinus's insights into his own literary and philosophical project, and he makes a compelling case for the predominance of ancient over modern influences on that project, though he occasionally misidentifies the latter.[35] Despite these findings, Walker's final assessment of Camus' effort is that by the time *Nuptials* appears in 1938, all that was left of Plotinus in this effort were his "key terms of reference," *patrie* and *exil*.[36] The principal feature of Plotinus's thought illuminated by these terms, his notion of the Ideal or transcendence, is completely absent. "By this time, Camus had completely rejected any vestige of belief in Plotinus' world of the Ideal or man's surviving link with it, the soul."[37] What Walker does not point out is that Camus himself was well aware of the ongoing debate regarding the transcendence or immanence of Plotinus's notion of the One.[38] Camus, for his part, came down on the side of immanence.[39] However, he did not do so uncritically. He added an important proviso to his interpretation: the use of terms like *transcendence* and *immanence* to explain Plotinus's thought, though perhaps inevitable, is nonetheless highly misleading because such terms employ spatial categories to elucidate what is essentially an "attempt at non-spatial thought."[40] This is a much more nuanced interpretation of Plotinus than the one with which Walker credits Camus. It suggests that once the metaphysics are set aside,

35. Walker says that Schopenhauer still belongs in some measure to the ancient world because he retains the notion of the Ideal (though he separates it too definitively from the real). However, he suggests that because Nietzsche has "no conception of the Ideal" his departure from the ancients is complete (830). I think it is open to question whether having or not having an Ideal in Walker's sense is the best way to determine one's relationship or lack thereof to the ancients.

36. Walker, "Camus, Plotinus, and 'Patrie,'" 839.

37. Ibid., 838.

38. Camus, *Essais*, 1284. Camus identifies the two styles of interpretation by their representatives: Caird for the notion of transcendence, and Zeller for the idea of Plotinian pantheism.

39. Ibid. "In our view, God is therefore immanent. Desire demands it. And furthermore, we carry within ourselves the three hypostases, since it is through inner mediation that we attain ecstasy and Union with the One."

40. Ibid., 1285.

Camus' nonspatial or existential use of Plotinian terms such as *patrie* and *exil* in his early works might be much more in accord with the spirit of Plotinus than Walker seems to allow.

Jacques Hardré's paper, "Camus' Thoughts on Christian Metaphysics and Neoplatonism," is more or less a summary of some of the principal themes of *Christian Metaphysics and Neoplatonism*. Hardré argues that this book, which had been largely ignored by commentators, helps to correct the popular opinion that Camus was uninterested in and unsympathetic to Christianity. *Christian Metaphysics* "shows very definitely the interest that the young Camus had in the development of early Christian thought and in the influence on this development of late Greek philosophy."[41] It is also a sound piece of scholarship. The text offers "clear proof that when Camus was later to write his commentaries on Christianity and on the Hellenistic spirit, he was doing so armed with knowledge acquired by careful and thorough research."[42] This does not mean that Camus' scholarship was original or groundbreaking, however. Hardré says that what *Christian Metaphysics* amounts to is not "a piece of original research but rather . . . a well-documented presentation of some aspects of a problem which has attracted many philosophers and theologians."[43] The real insight that the book affords us concerns what Camus thought about Christianity and Hellenism and the complex relationship between them.

I think Hardré's most important contribution to Camus scholarship is a political one. Against the current climate of opinion, he sought to make it clear to contemporary readers that Camus was not an illiterate modern whose rejection of Christianity was as ill-informed as it was unshakable. If Camus finally refused to accept the Christian faith, he did so only after giving it a patient and sympathetic hearing. Hardré also wanted to shore up the idea of Camus' Greek culture. It is true that commentators frequently speak of Camus' Hellenism and his affinity with classical Greece, but such remarks are often little more than lip service paid to popular opinion. Hardré wants to show that Camus' Hellenism was based on real research and not hastily gathered from an impressionistic reading in the tradition.

41. Hardré, "Camus' Thoughts," 97.
42. Ibid., 98.
43. Ibid.

I am sympathetic to Hardré's reading of *Christian Metaphysics*. The attribution to Camus either of a cliché or unreflective Hellenism or a thoughtless modernism has been equally obfuscating regarding his real achievement. Hardré's essay goes some way to overcoming both misconceptions, but there is still work to be done to complete the project. What is necessary is a thorough analysis aimed at explaining the manner in which these ideas, first developed in a coherent way in *Christian Metaphysics,* were worked out in Camus' later books. This is a task of which Hardré is aware but to which he only gestures in his article.

In *Camus' Hellenic Sources,* Paul Archambault undertakes to complete the task suggested by Hardré's study. He confirms Hardré's claim that little serious research has been devoted either to exploring Camus' Hellenism or to assessing his interpretation of Christianity, and he shares Hardré's opinion that the former has rarely been seriously questioned by scholars.[44] But that is where their agreement ends. Archambault's conclusions regarding *Christian Metaphysics* are the opposite of Hardré's, and he argues that the character of Camus' account of these subjects did not improve substantially in subsequent books.[45] Archambault argues that Camus' acquaintance with the texts and traditions of classical antiquity was neither extensive nor deep. He tries to demonstrate, popular opinion notwithstanding, that Camus' concerns were far more modern and Christian than Greek.[46]

Before discussing the main features of Archambault's critique, a word about the structure of his book is in order. His analysis is much more

44. Archambault, *Camus' Hellenic Sources,* 12.

45. Ibid., 13. Archambault claims that his analysis reveals that there is no significant development in Camus' thinking about the Greeks and Christians over the course of his entire career. "Taken on the whole . . . Hellenism and Christianity (as well as other related terms) meant much the same to [Camus] in 1960 as in 1936." Though the absence of change in Camus' account would be no objection in itself, Archambault's highly critical assessment of early books like *Christian Metaphysics* renders the claim anything but flattering. Be that as it may, the claim is rather odd because at the end of his study Archambault seems to make the opposite argument: "There is a marked progression from the uncritical, somewhat sophomoric repetition of Nietzsche's ideas on Greek tragedy in the *Essay on Music* (1932), and the mature lecture on *The Future of Tragedy* (1995), which, however derivative, shows signs of reflection and a fresh study of the primary sources" (ibid., 171).

46. "If it be a Christian disease to feel dispossessed and cast adrift in a hostile universe, it is fair to say that, although Camus fought that disease tooth and nail, he never entirely convalesced" (ibid., 104). And: "Camus, in short, cannot be considered as a Greek, but as a modern with a Greek heart who has been compelled to face the historical paradox of Christianity" (ibid., 173).

extensive and its consequences more far-reaching than those of Walker or Hardré, so a more detailed discussion is necessary to clarify his argument. Archambault orders the chapters of his book according to the broad historical periods apparent in Camus' sources. His aim is to determine the nature and quality of Camus' acquaintance with each one. In each chapter, that analysis has three stages or parts, which follow one another more or less sequentially. The first stage involves a comparative study of sample passages from Camus' books and secondary sources devoted to the same ancient texts. The aim here is to point out the manner in which Camus used and abused those sources. Archambault does this, not maliciously, but with a serious purpose. He argues that in order to measure the character of Camus' love for the Greeks, we need to know the degree of his acquaintance with their highest literary and philosophical achievements. "If it is true, as Aristotle and Aquinas have said, that no love is possible without prior knowledge, it seems reasonable to assume that Camus' knowledge of Greek culture is a fair stick wherewith to measure the quality of his love, inasmuch as love can be measured."[47] The second stage is a straightforward interpretation of the essays, novels, and plays in which Camus' analysis draws on ancient texts and themes, whether Greek, Christian, or Gnostic. The third stage is Archambault's own critical assessment of the quality of those various analyses. Here he ceases to play the role of detective and tries instead to meet Camus on his own ground, as a thinker or philosopher.

I have found much of Archambault's comparative work helpful in tracking down Camus' references and clarifying the sources of passages that he misidentifies. His study also includes a good discussion of some of the writers who might have helped shape Camus' understanding of the ancient world. Archambault's type of research is extremely useful in determining the scholarly nature and value of a book. It can also deepen our understanding of a text by providing us with important insight into its historical and philosophical context. This type of insight will often shed light on the kinds of problems and influences with which an author is grappling in his effort to formulate his own account. Archambault's study does all of these things in relation to Camus' books generally and *Christian Metaphysics* particularly, and the results of his efforts are of much use, as far as they go.

47. Ibid., 12.

The main difficulty with this aspect of Archambault's analysis is that the standards he sets for the appropriate use of sources are so stringent that I doubt any writer, primary or secondary, could meet them and still claim to be thinking for himself. Even in cases where Camus is clearly relying on the work of others and also attempting to surpass their analyses, Archambault characterizes Camus' use of sources as so naïve and uncritical that he is often unaware that they lead him to contradictory conclusions.[48] Archambault argues that this is particularly true of *Christian Metaphysics,* which was written by a young Camus who perhaps did not have the intellectual background and resources to untangle the many competing and even contradictory accounts of his sources.[49] But he also argues that the same can be said of many of Camus' later, more mature works.[50] Thus does Camus' Hellenism become derivative, sophomoric, and untenable, and his critique of Christianity uncharitable and uninformed. This is Archambault's most damning claim, the one to which his study as a whole points: Camus' acquaintance with Greek philosophy and literature was too scant, too superficial, and too misrepresentative to allow us to speak about Greek culture or Hellenism in his case in any meaningful sense at all.[51]

There are good reasons to have reservations about Archambault's argument, the first of which is the most obvious: all writers use and are influenced by the work of other writers, and there are instances in which that influence is so deep and long-standing that it is a difficult business to determine where the influence ends and a writer's own insight begins. This is not an apology for intellectual dishonesty or for shoddy

48. See Archambault's discussion of Camus' use of Nietzsche and Berdiaev in *The Rebel,* ibid., 90–95.

49. Ibid., 75. "In a sense, Camus was the victim of his uncritical attitude towards his sources: his general vision of the Greek universe had been bequeathed to him by an ardent German Hellenist who loathed philologists, as well as by serene French philologists who looked askance at intuitive scholarship. It would have taken a most ingenious conductor to induce such a motley chorus to sing in unison."

50. Ibid. "Camus had neither the taste nor the experience required for such an adventure of the mind; and, though he did attain a more sophisticated comprehension of Greek culture in his later years, his total vision of Hellenism and Christianity is obscured by ambiguities and contradictions much like those that remain in the opening chapter of *Christian Metaphysics.*"

51. Ibid., 169. "It does seem questionable . . . whether Camus' Greek culture was either profound or accurate. His opinions of Homer, Aeschylus, and Plato are impressive neither for their precision nor for their critical acuity."

scholarship, but a fact that we likely ought to recognize with gratitude. It is also one to which I think most writers would readily assent, if only the cameras were turned off.

Second, Camus' extraordinary popularity and the pervasive sense on the part of his readers that something distinguished him from the usual run of modern and Christian critics alike is itself a good indication that there is more real content in his books than Archambault admits. Eric Voegelin describes Camus' popularity and the meaning of this sense rather well: "At more than one American university, I could observe that the imitation of Camus's meditation has become, for numerous students, the method of catharsis. In this way they rid themselves of the intellectual pressure of either the leftist ideologies or the neo-Thomists or existentialist theologians, according to their respective milieu."[52] Of course, popularity is not proof, and the fact that Camus was neither an existentialist nor a Thomist does not mean he was necessarily a Greek. But all the indicators suggest that he was unquestionably something other than modern or Christian; and given his own repeated affirmations and the judgment of his readers, Greek is an appellation that is perhaps not too wide of the mark in this respect. Moreover, Voegelin was not alone in his assessment of this aspect of Camus' work, particularly as it is expressed in *The Rebel*. While the brightest lights of the French literary and philosophical world were busy panning *The Rebel* as intellectually sophomoric and politically reactionary, a man like Martin Buber was writing to Camus to congratulate him on his remarkable achievement and to seek permission to have the book published in Hebrew "because of its importance for human life at this hour."[53] And Hannah Arendt for her part was sending Camus encouraging notes and commenting to others that he was by far and away the best man in France at the time.[54] Voegelin, Buber, and Arendt all had their own philosophical projects, each with its own emphases and differences. Yet they all sought to articulate an alternative to the modern project, and they all had reasons to hesitate over Christianity. The fact that they all

52. Eric Voegelin, *Anamnesis,* trans. Gerhart Niemeyer (Columbia: University of Missouri Press, 1978), 172.

53. Martin Buber, *The Letters of Martin Buber: A Life of Dialogue,* ed. Nahum N. Glatzer and Paul Mendes-Flohr, trans. Richard and Clara Winston and Harry Zohn (New York: Schocken Books, 1991), 568–69.

54. Todd, *Camus: A Life,* 307.

recognized Camus' effort as compatible with their own is telling in this regard. It is not proof either. But it is highly suggestive of the nature of Camus' accomplishment.

Finally, there are also reasons to question Archambault's substantial analysis of Camus' Hellenism and his assessment of Christianity. Archambault argues that the most distorting feature of Camus' account of the relationship between Greeks and Christians is his "innate gift or compulsion for reflecting in antithetical terms, particularly with regard to this historical problem."[55] A few pages later, Archambault repeats the claim and gives it more weight by listing and then discussing the various types of antitheses Camus finds between the two traditions. Archambault's formulation of these antitheses will be familiar to any student of Camus and any reader of current Camus scholarship: "Hellenism is rebellious, whereas Christianity is resigned; Hellenism is esthetic, whereas Christianity is moral; Hellenism is tragic, whereas Christianity is dramatic; Hellenism is 'natural,' whereas Christianity is 'historical.'"[56] Archambault adds important qualifications to these formulations and acknowledges that Camus himself hesitated about a number of them.[57] Nonetheless, he stands by his argument that this type of antithetical thinking is an essential feature of Camus' books and that it is responsible for much of what is distorting and misrepresenting in them regarding the Greeks and Christians.

This is an important but difficult matter to discuss, in part because such tendencies do exist in Camus, but also because the field is overladen with scholarship that has itself become an object of study with its own categories and concerns, many of which have little to do either with Camus or with the original texts. Nonetheless, a few brief remarks are possible here. In Archambault's view, Camus' tendency to think in antithetical terms makes the difference between the Greeks and Christians seem absolute when in fact it is not.[58] This in turn distorts both traditions. For Archambault's Camus, the Greeks inhabit a static universe, bereft of progress or movement, while the Christians abandon all sense of nature and natural limits in order to be caught up in the

---

55. Archambault, *Camus' Hellenic Sources,* 63.
56. Ibid., 76.
57. Ibid.
58. Archambault argues that Camus acquired this tendency from writers like Nietzsche and Rougier, particularly the latter's book on Celsus. Ibid., 63–64.

movement of a providential history. Stated in this way, the argument is certainly false. From Parmenides to Plato (to say nothing of Homer), the Greeks knew both that time or history exists and that there are things that move and things that do not; and anyone who reads Augustine or Saint Francis knows that Christians experience and love nature too.

There is no doubt that Camus did at times formulate the relationship between the Greeks and Christians in these or similar terms. But there is much more to Camus' argument than Archambault supposes. Why Archambault misses it is hard to say. It might be a question of intent.

A good deal of Archambault's critical analysis is devoted to teaching his readers the proper Christian account of the relationship between nature and history and nature and supernature rather than to interpreting Camus' complex but provocative argument.[59] Unlike Archambault, for Camus Christianity is the real source of this antithetical structure. Archambault himself is not unaware of the possibility. Shortly after charging Camus with the use of such a structure, he cites what is perhaps its most famous Christian expression, Tertullian's "What has Athens to do with Jerusalem?"[60] Although Camus was tempted by such antithetical formulations, particularly in *The Rebel,* there is good evidence in his books that he recognized their limitations and was working toward a better account. I turn to that account now.

The notion that positions or ideas are antithetical is of course nothing new historically, but the Christian formulation gives that notion a new meaning and a much harsher cogency. Christianity insists and has always insisted that its revelation offers a unique insight into the human condition that differs qualitatively from any account that preceded it. It is therefore both historical and apocalyptic in the strongest sense. Ancient Greek oppositions or antitheses worked differently. They always took place against an enormous backdrop of agreement and shared meaning. Another way to say this is that the ancients never allowed the

59. See his discussion of nature and history particularly, ibid., 90–95.
60. The original text is from Tertullian, *On Prescription against Heretics,* chap. 7, trans. P. Holmes, in *The Ante-Nicene Fathers,* ed. A. Roberts and J. Donaldson (Edinburgh: T & T Clark, 1870), 15:9. Archambault cites it from Camus, *Essais,* 1244. The full text in Camus reads as follows: "What indeed has Athens to do with Jerusalem? What concord is there between the Academy and the Church? . . . Away with all attempts to produce a mottled Christianity of Stoic, Platonic, and dialectic composition! We want no curious disputation after possessing Christ Jesus, no inquisition after enjoying the gospel."

self-affirmation or self-interest inherent in the assertion of their difference to eclipse their awareness of the profound sameness of all human things. In Christianity that restraint is severed.[61] Though the historical results of that severing were in no way inevitable or fixed (people could have simply chosen to ignore it), it is arguable that much of what we know as the modern project was informed and inspired by it. The political antithesis that today goes by the name of totalitarianism is fiercer and intellectually more rigid than anything the ancients imagined; and our antidotes to that fierceness and rigidity—deconstruction or postmodernity—are weaker and less discriminating than what the ancients proposed. All this I assert in Camus' name.

As I have said, there are also ambiguities in Camus' account. There are moments when he seems to accept the antithetical structure of the Christian account as a way of framing his discussion.[62] At such moments, the Greeks disappear from Camus' analysis as a genuine alternative and he instead vacillates awkwardly between the two contemporary poles of the antithesis—modernity and Christianity. When this happens, even the Christian and modern apocalyptic formulations begin to make their way back into the analysis. Once the antithesis is accepted, these outcomes are inevitable. Its either/or structure is inherently apocalyptic; and intellectually all one can do is to vacillate, because the structure of the problem makes any choice between modernity and Christianity inherently unstable. One rejects the untenable teachings of one tradition only to find oneself forced to accept those of the other. And in either case one is denied some essential feature of human life (e.g., goodness, meaning), because the antithetical structure leads one to believe that it is possessed solely by the other side.

One of the things that distinguishes Camus from other critics of the modern project is that he had the courage and the honesty to admit to

---

61. Camus, *The Rebel*, 27, 28.

62. Ibid., 288. This is most evident when Camus frames the rebel's principal task as one of attempting to hold together God and History, rather than choosing between them, as do both moderns and Christians. But this is merely the Christian account in secular dress, and it differs fundamentally from what Camus earlier says about the Greeks, for whom such a choice was meaningless. "Metaphysical rebellion [the choice between God and History] presupposes a simplified view of creation, which the Greeks could not have. For them there were not gods on one side and men on the other, but degrees that lead from the latter to the former. The idea of innocence opposed to culpability, the vision of a history epitomized entirely by the struggle between good and evil, was foreign to them" (Camus, *Essais*, 439–40).

his own complicity in its excesses and confusions. He also understood their true nature. He knew that what prevented him from seeing the things with which he was confronted aright was not an intellectual problem in the narrow sense, nor simply his time understood as an external force, but a spiritual or existential malady that existed in the world around him and also in him. The following passage from "Return to Tipasa" is a moving account of his participation in at least one aspect of that malady: "I live with my family, who believes it reigns over rich and hideous cities, built of stones and mists. Day and night it raises its voice, and everything yields beneath it while it bows down to nothing: it is deaf to all secrets. Its power sustains me and yet bores me, and I come to be weary of its cries. But its unhappiness is my own, we are of the same blood. I too am sick, and am I not a noisy accomplice who has cried out among the stones?"[63] I think that the real aim of Camus' work, which is evident in *Christian Metaphysics* and in everything Camus wrote subsequently, from the anti-utopian analysis of *The Myth of Sisyphus* to the critique of metaphysical rebellion in *The Rebel*, is a critical assessment of the apocalyptic or totalitarian orientation of modernity and an attempt to track the historical and existential origin of that orientation back to its true source.[64] In at least one instance, Archambault seems to concede that this may indeed have been Camus' primary ambition, if not his greatest success. "If it be a Christian disease to feel dispossessed and cast adrift in a hostile universe, it is fair to say that, although Camus fought that disease tooth and nail, he never entirely convalesced."[65] But Archambault quickly returns to the text of his argument, and instead accuses Camus of confusing Christianity's best and most philosophically sound insights regarding the human condition with the excesses of Gnosticism, excesses to which he says Camus himself was strangely attracted at the same time that he would have criticized their political and existential consequences.[66]

---

63. Camus, "Return to Tipasa," in *Lyrical and Critical Essays,* 171.

64. For a fuller analysis of these efforts as they are undertaken in *The Rebel,* see Srigley, "Eric Voegelin's Camus: The Limitations of Greek Myth in *The Rebel.*"

65. Archambault, *Camus' Hellenic Sources,* 104.

66. Ibid. "I am rather inclined to think, however, that his metaphysical malaise was more Gnostic than Christian, the product, as it were, of a Graeco-Christian germ."

Compared to Camus' other books, *Christian Metaphysics* is a minor though important work. Despite the remarkable maturity of its insight, the book was written when Camus was very young, and so bears the marks of youth. It was written in order to fulfill the requirements of a university degree, and is therefore limited by a scholarly aim and format that was not native to Camus' writing and which he would soon abandon. Perhaps most important, Camus himself did not prepare the manuscript for publication. This last limitation is one that applies to all posthumous publications of Camus' works, from his early essays and first novel to the initial installment of *The First Man.*[67]

These limitations notwithstanding, *Christian Metaphysics* is an important book. It adds significantly to our understanding of the highest reaches of Camus' philosophical ambition and the direction of his thought. Apart from its own content, that importance is attested to in two principal ways: Camus' abiding concern with the subject matter of *Christian Metaphysics,* which he explores both directly and indirectly in virtually all of his subsequent books; and his decision to make that subject the theme of his third proposed philosophical essay, tentatively titled "The Myth of Nemesis." I will discuss the argument of *Christian Metaphysics,* comment briefly on its relationship to two later essays, *The Myth of Sisyphus* and *The Rebel,*[68] and then say a few words about Camus' plan for "The Myth of Nemesis" as he describes it in his *Notebooks.*

Anyone who reads *Christian Metaphysics* is left with a number of conflicting impressions. There is an unmistakable sense throughout the work that Camus prefers the Greeks to the Christians. But there are also passages in the book, particularly in its final pages, in which he seems to favor Christianity, both as preferable in itself and as the only effective alternative to the modern project.[69] Apart from Camus' preferences, there are substantial conflicts in the analysis, too. For instance, at times Camus suggests that there is a longing for transcendence or God in the

---

67. Albert Camus, *Cahiers II: Youthful Writings.* Albert Camus, *A Happy Death,* trans. Richard Howard (New York: Vintage Books, 1973). Albert Camus, *The First Man,* trans. David Hapgood (Toronto: Alfred A. Knopf Canada, 1995).

68. A similar type of comparative analysis could be done just as well with Camus' fictional works, but that would require more textual analysis than is possible here. The common literary form and philosophical content of *Christian Metaphysics* and the essays lend themselves to this type of analysis and will make the discussion that much more economical in this regard.

69. Camus, *Essais,* 1310.

Greeks that is similar to the one found in Christianity. However, at other times he says that such a longing is foreign to the Greeks.[70] And though he sometimes argues that Christianity revives the Greeks' tragic sense of life, he also claims that its hope in God and its advocation of humble submission to the divine order effectively undermine that sense.[71] All these different assertions can be found in Camus' analysis. What are we to make of them?

Conflicting or contradictory accounts cannot be reconciled, and I will not attempt to do so in the case of *Christian Metaphysics*. However, such accounts are often very telling and sometimes reveal patterns that can teach us about the kinds of problems with which an author is grappling. This is true in the case of *Christian Metaphysics*. I think there are two distinct interpretations of Hellenism and Christianity in *Christian Metaphysics*. One of these interpretations is Greek, the other Christian, though even in the former case traces of Christianity's influence remain. I think the existence of these two conflicting accounts is evidence of both Camus' uneasiness about Christianity and his inability to escape its assumptions completely. Camus knew or sensed that the Greeks were different, that they were people who needed and should be heard on their own terms and who perhaps could help us better understand our troubles.[72] But the pressure exerted by Christianity and modernity was pervasive and deep, and Camus was not immune to it. *Christian Metaphysics* is Camus' first attempt to free himself from that pressure and to reach some decision about the Greeks and Christians. His achievement is the foundation on which his later books are constructed.

Sometimes Camus argues that the longing for fulfillment or a homeland of the soul is a fundamental and constant human desire. So too, he claims, are the kinds of experiences that provoke that desire—the sense of all that is hard and immovable and tragic in life. That is Camus' Greek account. When arguing in this way, Camus interprets Christianity as having revived that longing and that tragic sense in comparison to a Greek culture that had become decadent. This is also Nietzsche's argument in

70. Consider only Camus' introduction. In it he says both that the Greeks had a "real tradition" of this longing and that they denied that God or the supernatural exists. Ibid., 1226–27.

71. Ibid., 1309, 1298.

72. Camus makes a compelling case for the Greeks in this respect in his essay "Helen's Exile," in *Lyrical and Critical Essays*, 148–53.

The Birth of Tragedy. According to Nietzsche, the Greeks "knew and felt the terror and horror of existence."[73] But through the influence of Socrates and the advent of the "theoretical man," that tragic sense died. "Apollinian contemplation" and "Dionysian ecstasies" were then replaced by "cool, paradoxical thoughts" and "fiery effects," both of which mimic the original but lack its substance.[74] These later Greeks got their cheerfulness and tragedy on the cheap. And Nietzsche claims that in comparison to them, Christianity's principal innovation was to renew the spirit of the older Greeks in some measure: "It was this semblance of 'Greek cheerfulness' which so aroused the profound and formidable natures of the first four centuries of Christianity: this womanish flight from seriousness and terror, this craven satisfaction with easy enjoyment, seemed to them not only contemptible, but a specifically anti-Christian sentiment."[75]

Despite its favorable assessment of Christianity, Camus' interpretation rests on principles that are opposed to its self-understanding. According to that self-understanding, Christianity's insight into the human condition is absolutely unique and thus unprecedented historically. And although it entails suffering, its vision is not tragic in the Greek sense, because it promises a final liberation from the self and its attachment to the world, which is the cause of its suffering.[76] Camus' interpretation denies that uniqueness and the developmental history on which it rests. And when he applauds Christianity's renewal of tragedy, his compliment also contains a critique or insult, because it implies that Christianity's seriousness is to be measured by the extent to which it approximates the teachings of those from whom it most wished to distinguish itself, the Greeks.

As I have said, *Christian Metaphysics* also contains another, very different interpretation of the Greeks and Christians, one that belies an

---

73. Friedrich Nietzsche, *The Birth of Tragedy and The Case against Wagner,* trans. Walter Kaufmann (New York: Vintage Books, 1967), sect. 15.

74. Ibid., sect. 12.

75. Ibid., sect. 11.

76. Both aspects of the Christian teaching are nicely stated in the following passage from Bruce Ward and P. Travis Kroeker's book on Dostoevsky's prophetic Christianity: "Only by dying to the isolation of immanent earthly realism can one become alive to life itself and thus 'bear fruit.' It is a vision that reverses the cosmologies and ideologies of modernity no less than it did the expectations of Jews and Greeks in Jesus' time." Kroeker and Ward, *Remembering the End,* 20.

acceptance of Christianity's own self-understanding. In opposition to his Greek account, Camus here argues that the longing for a homeland of the soul is a desire that the Greeks did not experience, and indeed that their understanding of human life was constructed on assumptions that are inimical to such aspirations. He denies that the Greeks had any meaningful sense of the supernatural or God and therefore experienced no desire for a transcendent fulfillment comparable to the one we find in Christianity. Nor were they troubled by apocalyptic conceptions of history or the problem of human destiny. According to this account, the Greeks believe in a "cyclical world, eternal and necessary, which could not be reconciled with a creation *ex nihilo* and hence with an end of the world."[77] When Camus speaks about the Greeks in this way, there is no trace of the charge of decadence, nor does he say that their insight into human life has anything particularly tragic about it. These Greeks are cheerful and untroubled, to the extent of being satisfied with a "sportive and aesthetic justification of existence."[78]

Even though Camus is sympathetic to the Greeks understood in this way, the interpretation itself turns on assumptions inherent to the Christian historiography which are anything but sympathetic to the Greeks. It is a familiar argument to our modern ears: the Greeks have only reason and the mind, not spirit or soul; the Greeks have no sense of transcendence in the eminent sense as God, only the polytheistic and intercosmic gods of Olympus; the Greeks were too naïve to believe that human beings knowingly do wrong, and so understood neither sin nor evil. The general picture is one in which the Greeks were not morally serious.[79] Since they lacked Christianity's profound revelation concerning the human condition, they did not and could not understand the meaning of that condition's two gravest problems: suffering and death;[80] nor could they understand the pressing need for redemption.

77. Camus, *Essais*, 1226. Camus makes the same argument in *The Rebel:* "The Greek idea of evolution has nothing in common with our idea of historical evolution. The difference between the two is the difference between a circle and a straight line. The Greeks imagined the history of the world as cyclical. Aristotle, to give a definite example, did not believe that the time in which he was living was subsequent to the Trojan war" (189–90).

78. Camus, *Essais*, 1225.

79. This kind of argument was made popular in the modern period by Kierkegaard's work. For a clear statement of the argument, see Søren Kierkegaard, *The Sickness unto Death*, trans. Howard and Edna Hong (Princeton: Princeton University Press, 1980), 87–96.

80. Camus, *Essais*, 1225–26.

Though Camus' Greek account is better than his Christian account, both are hampered in some measure by Christian assumptions that distort the historical record and force Camus to solve Christian problems with Greek formulae.[81] But there are moments when Camus manages to break free of these Christian assumptions entirely. Then he offers a different interpretation of the Greeks and a very different critique of Christianity. "In this world, in which the desire for God is getting stronger, the problem of the Good loses ground."[82] This is a stunning remark. Here Camus makes it clear that the Christian longing for God or transcendence is not the same thing as the Greek aspiration to virtue, and that far from surpassing the Greeks in terms of its moral seriousness or courage, Christianity actually falls far short of their best insights and even diminishes the ancient and persistent human desire for the Good. This is an insight that is not limited by Christian assumptions, and it is not the only one of its kind in *Christian Metaphysics.*

Though Camus usually interprets the Greeks as having a purely rational conception of the world, one that is governed by logic in the narrow sense as the principle of noncontradiction, there are other instances in which he says that such an account distorts the true nature of reason.[83] This distorted reason turns on the assumption that truth and beauty are somehow opposed, and that so too are the human capacities by which they are apprehended. Camus claims that this opposition is not native to the

81. Ibid., 1251. This is the way Camus describes the role of the Gnostics in the evolution of Christian metaphysics: "Gnosticism poses problems in a Christian manner; it solves them in Greek formulas." This is an endless undertaking and a futile one, I think. There is no solution, Greek or otherwise, to a problem to which it is not addressed; and since in his best account Camus claims that many of the Christian problems he identifies are false or misleading, there can be no true solution to them.

82. Ibid., 1227.

83. This account of reason is apparent in the concluding remarks of Camus' chapter on Augustine: "At bottom the enigma is that this fusion had worked at all, because though the Greco-Roman world's sensibility was open to the Gospel, Reason itself refused to accept a certain number of postulates. Providentialism, creationism, philosophy of history, a taste for humility, all the themes that we have pointed out run counter to the Greek attitude. This Greek naïveté of which Schiller speaks was too full of innocence and light to abdicate without resistance. The task of the conciliators was to transform the very instrument of this attitude, that is to say, Reason, governed by the principle of contradiction, into a notion shaped by the idea of participation. Neoplatonism was the unconscious artisan of this reconciliation. But there is a limit to the flexibility of intelligence. And Greek civilisation, in the person of Plotinus, stopped halfway" (ibid., 1307).

Greeks, but rather was first introduced by Christianity: "For the Christian who separates Reason and Beauty, the Truth of Beauty, Reason is reduced to its role of logical legislator. And thus conflicts between Faith and Reason become possible. For a Greek, these conflicts are less acute, because Beauty, which is both order and sensitivity, economy and the object of passion, remains a ground of agreement."[84] This brief remark undermines the Christian notion of an opposition between faith and reason, the heart and the mind, and thereby also one of the most common ways in which the Greeks are misinterpreted today, whether one does so with approbation or disapproval.

I do not think that the competing interpretations of the Greeks and Christians apparent in *Christian Metaphysics* are due to Camus' uncritical appropriation of conflicting literary sources, as Archambault claims. Rather, I think they are provoked by Camus' serious engagement with the subject and his attempt to overcome certain Christian and modern assumptions about the nature of the Greeks and the role of Christianity in the advent of modernity. Even in this early book Camus is asking the right questions, and against the habits of his time he demonstrates a remarkable sense of what is at stake in the quarrel between the ancients and the moderns.

Camus' concern with the relationships between the Greeks, Christians, and moderns continues in his later works, particularly in his two book-length essays, *The Myth of Sisyphus* and *The Rebel*. It is arguable that in this period of Camus' career, say roughly from 1943 to 1953, these relationships are his principal concern. But the manner in which he addresses them changes, as do the kinds of problems he confronts and the solutions he proposes. Over the course of his career, Camus attempted a number of different ways of distinguishing between the Greeks and the Christians, each with its own set of problems and its own contradictions. If there is one thing that is common in his work in this respect, it is this pattern. The pattern also has another feature. In subsequent books, the contradictions continue to work in much the same way that they do in *Christian*

---

84. Ibid., 1272. Although this analysis takes place in the context of a discussion of Plotinus's role in the evolution of Christian metaphysics, which was to soften the notion of reason into the notion of participation, it is clear that Camus is here speaking about an older Greek tradition.

Metaphysics. In each case, there is a predominately Greek approach to the subject that exists uneasily alongside an essentially Christian approach. What defines both traditions in each new formulation differs, of course. But the pattern itself remains the same.

In *The Myth of Sisyphus,* the Greek aspect of Camus' analysis is apparent in his highly critical assessment of Christian and modern apocalyptic aspirations and in his attempt to formulate his own interpretation of the absurd or modern nihilism.[85] But there is a reverse side to Camus' critique that belies acceptance of at least one feature of the Christian teaching. Although Camus argues that our modern sense of meaninglessness is not due to the loss of an apocalyptic fulfillment in either the Christian or the modern sense, his critically clarified account of the absurd constantly threatens to teeter into nihilism for precisely this reason. There is an abiding sense in *The Myth of Sisyphus* that without the final reckoning entailed by such a fulfillment, morality and goodness are groundless.

In one formulation, Camus interprets Christian and modern apocalyptic constructions and their derivations as pseudo-problems to be rejected outright in favor of an entirely different kind of interpretation. In another formulation, those constructions, despite Camus' critical analysis, somehow remain the measure of truth in such matters. The periodic denials of all value and meaning in *The Myth of Sisyphus* are typical in this regard.[86] Camus never says these things in so many words, of course, and there is ample evidence in the book that he is uneasy with this conclusion. Nonetheless, the contradiction exists, and a lack of clarity about its character is responsible for a good deal of the scholarly confusion about the nature of Camus' achievement.

In *The Rebel,* such contradictions become even more explicit even while they are formulated in different terms. Archambault and others like to point out the difficulties surrounding Camus' use of nature and history as means of distinguishing between the Greeks and Christians.

---

85. See my unpublished manuscript, "Albert Camus's Absurd Man: A Reconsideration of *The Myth of Sisyphus,*" 6–16.

86. Albert Camus, *The Myth of Sisyphus,* trans. Justin O'Brien (London: Penguin Books, 1988), 53, 59. The following two texts are exemplary in this regard: "At this point the problem is reversed. It was previously a question of finding out whether or not life had to have a meaning to be lived. It now becomes clear on the contrary that it will be lived all the better if it has no meaning." "Once and for all, value judgements are discarded here in favour of factual judgements."

There are such difficulties in the text, but they are by no means the most basic or the most important ones. *The Rebel* is a history, a history of rebellion and its role in the advent of the modern Western world. The most provocative and contradictory feature of Camus' analysis is his history of antiquity. To state the matter simply, the primary contradiction in Camus' ancient history lies in his conflicting interpretation of Christianity. This contradiction also plays itself out backward and forward into conflicting interpretations of the Greeks and the Jews on the one hand, and of modernity on the other. I think there are two distinct patterns that emerge from these conflicting interpretations. These patterns amount to two different histories of antiquity, histories that in turn result in two very different interpretations and assessments of modernity. One history is Greek, the other Christian. In the former history, Camus argues that Christianity and modernity are the same thing. Christianity has no answer to the crisis of the modern world, particularly its most extreme or totalitarian manifestation, that is not itself an earlier expression of the same pathology. Here Camus proposes the Greeks as the only real alternative to modernity, not because their account solves Christian and modern problems, but because it recognizes them to be false and thus as insoluble on their own terms.

The findings of Camus' Greek history are contradicted by those of his Christian history. In the latter, Camus claims that our current forms of metaphysical rebellion began historically not with Christianity but with Judaism. Here Camus argues that Christianity successfully overcame the problems from which metaphysical rebellion arises. These are the problems of "evil and death," which, though constant in human life, had been exacerbated in the West by the Jewish invention of a radically transcendent personal God who is somehow responsible for everything but whose ways do not correspond to any normal human judgment about what is good and what evil.[87] The sole textual evidence that Camus offers in support of this claim is the story of Cain and Abel, in which God prefers the latter's sacrifice to the former's "without any convincing motive . . . and, by so doing, provokes the first murder."[88] Nonetheless, he argues that herein lies the real source of our contemporary history. "The history of rebellion, as we are experiencing it today, has far more to do with the

---

87. Camus, *The Rebel*, 32.
88. Ibid., 33.

children of Cain than with the disciples of Prometheus. In this sense it is the God of the Old Testament who is primarily responsible for mobilizing the forces of rebellion."[89]

Here Camus interprets Christianity, not the Greeks, as the most effective alternative to modernity, because it is the only tradition to have overcome the metaphysical rebellion on which modernity rests. The Greeks are given a vastly subordinate role. They contribute the notion of mediation, which on its own solves nothing, but when adopted by Christianity is deepened into the notion of incarnation and then used as a means of overcoming Judaism's radical separation of God and world. And when it comes to Camus' own formulation of the type of rebellion that might avoid the excesses of modern metaphysical rebellion while retaining the necessary willingness to resist, the account he offers is remarkably similar in both form and content to the Christian account. "There is in fact no conciliation between a god who is totally separated from history and a history purged of all transcendence. Their representatives on earth are, indeed, the yogi and the commissar. . . . Between God and history, the yogi and the commissar, [rebellion] opens a difficult path where contradictions may exist and thrive."[90] Despite its modern philosophical language and the reference to Koestler's book, what else is this but a reformulation of the Christian notion of incarnation? *The Rebel* does not leave most readers with the impression that Camus was particularly sympathetic to Christianity or that he endorsed it as a viable alternative to the modern project. But in at least one version of Camus' history Christianity does just that. I think Camus was aware of the limitations of his analyses in *The Myth of Sisyphus* and *The Rebel*—perhaps not in all their details, and perhaps not of the fact that they point to contradictions of the type that I have described here. But he knew that something was amiss or incomplete, the best evidence of which is his proposed third philosophical essay.

Camus ordered his books very carefully. The well-known three-cycle structure of his works was first formulated in 1947 and achieved its final form in 1955.[91] According to that structure, "The Myth of Nemesis" is

89. Ibid., 32.
90. Ibid., 288, 290.
91. Camus, *Notebooks 1942–1951,* 158. Albert Camus, *Carnets III: mars 1951–décembre 1959* (Paris: Éditions Gallimard, 1989), 187. When I say "final form" I mean last. What Camus would have done with the structure had he lived is a matter of speculation.

the name Camus gives to the third of these cycles, the familiar *Myth of Sisyphus* and *Myth of Prometheus* being those given to the first two, respectively.[92] In a subsequent reference to the Nemesis cycle, Camus gives the theme a content: "Go back to the passage from Hellenism to Christianity, the true and only turning point in history."[93] Five years later, he continued to explore the same historical problematic, only this time as a means of explaining certain features of the modern world. In 1957 he writes: "Nemesis: The profound complicity between Marxism and Christianity (to develop). That is why I am against them both."[94] And a year later, in April 1958, he states his own positive ambition explicitly: "The world marches toward paganism, but again it rejects pagan values. We must restore them. We must paganize belief, grecesize the Christ and restore balance."[95]

The proposed subject of the Nemesis cycle is the subject of *Christian Metaphysics and Neoplatonism.* It would seem that the basic idea had remained unchanged for Camus over the course of more than twenty years. Indeed, his books and notebooks indicate that as Camus matured he became even more convinced of the importance of that historical dispensation, particularly for his own attempt to understand the course of the modern world as it races toward perfect justice and perfect freedom. In a sense, Camus never ceased to address the problem he first explored in *Christian Metaphysics.* That problem or question concerns the nature of the Greeks, how Christianity departs from their insights and their ways of life, and how that departure and its extraordinary influence have contributed to the advent of the modern world. All these elements can be found in one form or other in *Christian Metaphysics;* and they can also be found, whether as buried themes or as explicit analyses, in virtually all of Camus' subsequent books. I hope the publication of this translation will encourage Camus' readers to consider them afresh. I think that Camus still has much to teach us in this regard.

92. Camus, *Notebooks 1942–1951*, 257.
93. Ibid., 267.
94. Camus, *Carnets III*, 209.
95. Ibid., 220.

Christian
Metaphysics
and
Neoplatonism

Introduction

In the paintings of the Catacombs, the Good Shepherd often assumes the face of Hermes. But if the smile is the same, the symbol has changed its significance. It is in this manner that Christian thought, constrained to express itself in a coherent system, attempted to adopt Greek thought forms and to express itself in the metaphysical formulas that it found ready-made. Nevertheless it transformed them. Hence in order to understand the originality of Christianity, it is necessary to clarify that which constitutes its profound meaning, and from a historical point of view to go back to its sources. This is the goal of the present work. But any research, to be coherent, must organize itself according to one or two fundamental approaches. This introduction will permit us to define these approaches, to the extent that, considering the complexity of the historical materials that concern us, it will nevertheless underscore in them certain constant elements.

It has often been asked what constitutes the originality of Christianity in relation to Hellenism. In addition to the evident differences, a good number of themes remain common. But to tell the truth, in all cases where a civilization is born—the great affair of humanity—we observe a changing of planes and not a substitution of systems. It is not by comparing Christian dogmas and Greek philosophy that we can get some idea of that which separates them, but rather by observing that the sentimental plane, where the Evangelical communities were situated, is foreign to the classic aspect of Greek sensibility. It is on the affective plane where problems arise and not in the system that tries to respond to them that we ought to find what made Christianity novel. In its beginnings,

Christianity is not a philosophy that is opposed to a philosophy, but an ensemble of aspirations, a faith, that moves to a certain plane and seeks its solutions within that plane.

But it is here, before speaking about what is irreducible in the two civilizations, that it is appropriate to introduce certain nuances and to keep in mind the complexity of the problem. It is always arbitrary to speak of a "Greek spirit" as opposed to a "Christian spirit." Æschylus along with Sophocles, the primitive masks and the Panathénées, the lecythes of the fifth century alongside the metopes of the Parthenon, and finally the mysteries as well as Socrates, all incline to emphasize next to the Greece of light a Greece of darkness, which is less classic but just as real. But on the other hand, it goes without saying that one can draw out of a civilization a certain number of favorite themes and, with the assistance of Socratism, trace within Greek thought a certain number of privileged images, the composition of which inspires precisely what one calls Hellenism. Something in Greek thought prefigures Christianity, while something else rejects it in advance.

a) *The Differences.* It is possible in this manner to identify among Greeks and Christians irreconcilable attitudes before the world. As it is expressed in the first centuries of our era, Hellenism implies that man can be self-sufficient and that he has within himself the means to explain the universe and destiny. Its temples are constructed to its measure. In a certain sense, the Greeks accepted a sportive and æsthetic justification of existence. The line of their hills, or the run of a young man on a beach, provided them with the whole secret of the world. Their gospel said: our Kingdom is of this world. Think of Marcus Aurelius's "Everything is fitting for me, my Universe, which fits thy purpose."[1] This purely rational conception of life—in which the world can be understood completely—leads to a moral intellectualism: virtue is a thing that

---

1. *Pensées* IV, 23: "Tout ce qui t'accommode, Cosmos, m'accommode: rien n'est prématuré ou tardif de ce qui pour toi échoit à son heure; je fais mon fruit de ce que portent les saisons, ô nature. De toi naît tout, en toi est tout, vers toi va tout."

["Everything is fitting for me, my Universe, which fits thy purpose. Nothing in thy good time is too early or too late for me; everything is fruit for me which thy seasons, Nature, bear; from thee, in thee, to thee are all things." Marcus Aurelius, *Meditations* 4.23, in *The Meditations of Marcus Aurelius Antoninus,* trans. A. S. L. Farquharson (Oxford: Oxford University Press, 1989), 27–28.—Trans.]

is learned. Without always acknowledging it, all Greek philosophy makes its sages God's equals. And God being nothing more than a higher science, the supernatural does not exist: the whole universe is centered around man and his endeavors. If, therefore, moral evil is ignorance[2] or error, how do the notions of Redemption and Sin fit into this attitude?

As to the rest and in the physical order, the Greeks still believed in a cyclical world, eternal and necessary, which could not be reconciled with a creation *ex nihilo*[3] and hence with an end of the world.[4]

Generally speaking, because they were attached to the reality of the pure idea, the Greeks could not understand the dogma of a bodily resurrection. The mockery of Celsus, Porphyry, and Julian, for example, is endless in regard to this idea. Therefore whether in physics, in morality, or in metaphysics, the differences lay in the way the problems were posed.

But at the same time, some positions remained similar. Neither Neoplatonism, which is the ultimate effort of Greek thinking, nor Christianity can be understood without considering the substance of the common aspirations, to which all thought of this epoch must respond.

---

2. Cf. Epictetus *Moral Discourses* 1, 7: "If you cannot correct the wicked, do not blame them, for all wickedness is correctable; but instead blame yourself, you who cannot find in yourself enough eloquence or perseverance to lead them to the good."
[I have been unable to find in Epictetus's text the passage to which Camus here refers. In lieu of a standard English translation of the primary text, I have therefore provided an English translation of Camus' French text. All such subsequent translations will be indicated by asterisk.—Trans.]

3. ["out of nothing"—Trans.]

4. Cf. Aristotle *Probl.* XVIII, 3 [*sic*]: "Si la suite des événements est un cercle, comme le cercle n'a ni commencement ni fin, nous ne pouvons, par une plus grande proximité à l'égard du commencement, être antérieur à ces gens-là [les contemporains de la guerre de Troie] et ils ne peuvent pas non plus être antérieurs à nous."
[Cf. Aristotle *Problems* 17.3: "If, then, there is a circle, and a circle has neither beginning nor end, men would not be 'before' [the contemporaries of the war of Troy] because they are nearer the beginning, nor should we be 'before' them, nor they 'before' us." *Aristotle: Problems*, vol. 1, ed. T. E. Page, trans. W. S. Hett, Loeb Classical Library (Cambridge: Harvard University Press, 1936), 367. In *The Rebel*, Camus cites the same passage from Aristotle in order to distinguish between Christian and Greek accounts of history: "The Greek idea of becoming has nothing in common with our idea of historical evolution. The difference between the two is the difference between a circle and a straight line. The Greeks imagined the history of the world as cyclical. Aristotle, to give a definite example, did not believe that the time in which he was living was subsequent to the Trojan War." Camus, *The Rebel*, trans. Anthony Bower (New York: Vintage Books, 1991), 189–90. I have rendered *devenir* as "becoming" rather than "evolution," as in Bower's translation. The translation is more literal and closer, I believe, to Camus' meaning.—Trans.]

b) *The Common Aspirations.* Few periods were as distressed as that one. In an extraordinary incoherence of races and peoples, the ancient Greco-Roman themes were mixed with this new wisdom that came from the Orient. Asia Minor, Syria, Egypt, and Persia were sending thoughts and thinkers to the Western world.[5] The lawyers of the time were Ulpian of Tyre and Papinian of Herese. Ptolemy and Plotinus were Egyptians; Porphyry and Iamblicus, Syrians; Diasconides and Galen, Asians. Lucian himself, that consecrated "attic" spirit, is from Commagene at the frontier of the Euphrates. And it is in this manner that in the same epoch the heavens could be populated by the gnostic Æons, the Jewish Yahweh, the Christian Father, the Plotinian One, and the old Roman gods themselves, still worshiped in the Italian countryside.

And certainly one can find political and social causes for this state of affairs: cosmopolitanism[6] or real economic crises of the epoch. But it is also that a certain number of passionate demands begin to be born that will attempt to satisfy themselves at all cost. And the Orient is not alone responsible for this awakening. If it is true, then, that Greece euhemerised[7] the gods, if it is true that the problem of the destiny of the soul had disappeared beneath Epicurean and Stoic ideas, it nonetheless remains true that the Greco-Roman world was returning to a real tradition. But something new is nevertheless making itself felt.

In this world, in which the desire for God is getting stronger, the problem of the Good loses ground. For the pride of life that animated the ancient world, this new world substituted the humility of spirits in pursuit of inspiration. The æsthetic plane of contemplation is concealed by the tragic plane where hopes are limited to the imitation[8] of a God.

---

5. Cf. Cumont, *Les Religions orientales dans le paganisme romain.*

6. Alexander, in his campaigns in the Orient, had created more than forty Greek cities.

7. Euhemerised: a neologism derived from Euhemer, a Greek mythographer for whom the gods were human beings, deified through the belief of their fellow men. (R. Q.)

[A note by Roger Quilliot, editor of the Pléiade edition of Camus' collected works.—Trans.]

8. Cf. "L'homme nouveau" dans les rites de purification à Éleusis: "La déesse Brimo a enfanté Brimos" *Philosoph.:* V.8. Cf. Plutarque, *de Iside,* 27, according to Loisy, *Les mystères païens et le mystère chrétien,* ch. IV, p. 139 [*sic*]: "Après avoir comprimé et étouffé la rage de Typhon [Iside] ne voulut pas que les combats qu'elle avait soutenus . . . tombassent dans l'oubli et le silence. Elle institua donc initiations très simples où seraient représentées par des images, des allégories et par des scènes figurées les souffrances de sa lutte."

[Cf. *The New Man* in the rites of purification at Eleusis: "The goddess Brimo gave birth to Brimos." *Philosoph.* 5.8.* Cf. Plutarch *De Iside et Osiride* 27: "The sister and wife of Osiris,

They act out the sorrowful drama of Isis in search of Osiris;[9] they die with Dionysius,[10] and they are reborn with him. Attis is subjected to the worst mutilations.[11] In Eleusis,[12] Zeus is united with Demeter in the person of the great priest and hierophant.

And in the same period, there infiltrates Lucretius's idea that the world is not oriented toward the "all things are the same forever,"[13] but that it serves as the scene for the tragedy of man without God. The problems themselves are incarnated, and the philosophy of history is born. One will be less reluctant consequently to accept this change of the world that constitutes Redemption. It is not a matter of knowing or of understanding, but of loving. And Christianity can do nothing but embody this idea, so little Greek in nature, that the problem for man is not to perfect his nature, but to escape it. The desire for God, humility, imitation, and aspirations toward a rebirth, all these themes are intertwined in the Oriental mysteries and religions of Mediterranean paganism. Above all, since the second century before Christ (the cult of Cybele was introduced in Rome in 205 BCE), the principal religions have not ceased, in their influence and in their expansion, to prepare the way for Christianity. In the period that concerns us, new problems are posed in all their acuteness.

c) *The Position of the Problem and the Plan of This Work.* To consider Christianity as a new form of thought that suddenly overtook Greek civilization would therefore be to evade the difficulties. Greece is continued in Christianity. And Christianity is prefigured in Hellenic thought.

-----

however, as his helper quenched and stopped Typho's mad frenzy, nor did she allow the contests and struggles which she had undertaken . . . to be engulfed in oblivion and silence, but into the most sacred rites she infused images, suggestions and representations of her experiences at that time, and so she consecrated at once a pattern of piety and an encouragement to men and women overtaken by similar misfortunes." *Plutarch's De Iside et Osiride*, ed. and trans. J. Gwyn Griffiths (Wales: University of Wales Press, 1970), 159. In Loisy, the first sentence of this passage actually reads: "après avoir comprimé et étouffé la folie et la rage de Typhon."—Trans.]

9. Cf. Loisy, [*Les mystères païens et le mystère chrétien,*] ch. I.

10. Cf. Cumont, [*Les Religions orientales,*] appendix: "Les Mystères de Bacchus."

11. Ibid., ch. III.

12. Loisy, [*Les mystères païens et le mystère chrétien,*] ch. II.

13. ["Sunt eadem (*sic*) omnia semper." Camus offers no reference for this passage. The text is from Lucretius *De Rerum Natura* 1.945. It should read "eadem sunt omnia semper." Lucretius, *De Rerum Natura,* trans. William Ellery Leonard (New York: E. P. Dutton, 1916).—Trans.]

It is far too easy to see in dogmatic Christianity a Greek addition that nothing in the evangelical doctrines could legitimate. But on the other hand, one cannot deny the Christian contribution to the thought of the period, and it seems difficult to exclude all notion of a Christian philosophy.[14] One thing is common, and it is an anxiety that gave birth to problems: it is an identical evolution that leads from the practical concerns of Epictetus to the speculations of Plotinus and from the inward Christianity of Paul to the dogmatism of the Greek Fathers. But can we distinguish, nevertheless, even in this confusion, what constitutes Christianity's originality? There is the whole problem.

From a historical point of view, Christian doctrine is a religious movement, born in Palestine, and inscribed in Jewish thought. In a period that is difficult to determine, but certainly contemporary with the moment when Paul authorized in principle the admission of gentiles and exempted them from circumcision,[15] Christianity was separated from Judaism. At the end of the first century, John proclaimed the identity of the Lord and the Spirit. The Epistle of Barnabas, written between 117 and 130 CE, is already resolutely anti-Jewish. This is the fundamental point. Christian thought is then separated from its origins and is dispersed throughout the entire Greco-Roman world. The Greco-Roman world, prepared by its anxieties and by mystery religions, ended by accepting Christianity.

We are not interested, consequently, in separating absolutely the two doctrines, but rather in discovering how they have united their efforts and in seeing what, in each of them, has remained intact in this collaboration. But what Ariadne's thread must we follow to find our way through this confusion of ideas and systems? Let us say at once that what constitutes the irreducible originality of Christianity is the theme of Incarnation. The problems are made flesh and immediately assume the tragic and necessary character that is so often absent from certain games of the Greek spirit. Even after the Jews had rejected and the Mediterraneans accepted Christianity, its profoundly innovative character survived. And Christian thought, which inevitably borrows formulas ready-made from the philosophy of the time, transfigures these

---

14. *Bulletin de la Société française de Philosophie,* March 1931. *Revue de métaphysique et de morale* (Bréhier) April 1931; ibid. (Souriau), July 1932.
15. That is to say, near the middle of the first century.

formulas nevertheless. The role of Greece was to universalize Christianity by orienting it toward metaphysics. The mysteries and an entire tradition that finds its source in Æschylus and the Doric Apollos had prepared it for this role. In this manner, a movement is explained in which the Christian miracle had known to assimilate into itself the Greek miracle and to discard the bases of a civilization sufficiently durable that we are still permeated by it today.

Our task and our plan are thus outlined: to observe in Neoplatonism the effort of Greek philosophy to give the problem of the period a specifically Hellenic solution, to trace the Christian attempt to adapt its dogma to its primitive religious life, just at the moment when, encountering in Neoplatonism metaphysical structures already formed out of a religious thought, Christianity blossoms in the second revelation that was Augustinian thought. But there are three stages or moments in the evolution of Christianity: Evangelical Christianity, in which it finds its source; dogmatic Augustinianism, in which it achieved the reconciliation of the Word and the flesh; and the intervals in which it allowed itself to be led to attempt to identify knowledge and salvation, that is to say, the heresies of which Gnosticism offers a complete example. Gospel, Gnosis, Neoplatonism, and Augustinianism: we will study these four stages of one common Greco-Christian evolution, in historical order and in the relation they maintain with the movement of thought in which they are joined. Evangelical Christianity spurned all speculation but asserted, since the beginning, the themes of Incarnation; Gnosis sought a special solution in which Redemption and knowledge are joined; and Neoplatonism endeavored to achieve its purposes by attempting to reconcile rationalism and mysticism and, with the assistance of its formulas, permitted dogmatic Christianity to form itself, through Saint Augustine, into a metaphysics of Incarnation. At the same time, Neoplatonism served here as a control-doctrine. The movement that animates it is the same one that drives Christian thought, but the notion of Incarnation remained foreign to it.

Already by the sixth century, this movement is consummated: "Neoplatonism dies with all Greek philosophy and culture: the sixth and seventh centuries are periods of great silence."[16]

---

16. Émile Bréhier, *Histoire de la philosophie I*, II, ch. VII, p. 484.

Chapter One

Evangelical Christianity

It is difficult to speak as a whole of an "Evangelical Christianity." Nevertheless, it is possible to discern in it a certain state of mind in which the later evolution has its source. The favored theme, that one which is at the center of Christian thought at the time and around which everything converges, the natural solution to the aspirations of the period, is the Incarnation. The Incarnation, that is to say, the meeting of the divine and the flesh in the person of Jesus Christ; the extraordinary adventure of a God taking responsibility for the sin and the misery of man, the humility and the humiliations, are presented as so many symbols of Redemption. But this notion crowns a group of aspirations that it is incumbent upon us to define.

There are two states of mind in the Evangelical Christian: pessimism and hope. Evolving toward a certain tragic plane, humanity at that time relied only on God and, entrusting into his hands all hope of a better destiny, longed only for him, saw only him in the Universe, abandoned all interests apart from faith, and incarnated in God the very symbol of this restlessness so divided from spiritual aspirations. One must choose between the world and God. These are the two aspects of Christianity that we will have to examine successively in the first part of this chapter. The study of the milieu and the literature of the period will then display for us these different themes among the men of Evangelical Christianity.

The most reliable method is to go back to the New Testament texts themselves. But a supplementary method consists in appealing, whenever it is possible, to a pagan polemicist.[1] Their reproaches, in effect, give us a sufficiently exact idea of what, in Christianity, would offend a Greek, and thus leave us well informed about the novelty of the former's contribution.

I. The Themes of Evangelical Christianity

A. *The Tragic Plane*

Ignorance and disdain of all systematic speculation, these are what characterize the state of mind of the first Christians. The facts blind them and press them, especially the fact of death.

a) At the end of the fourth century, Julius Quintus-Hilarianus, bishop of the African proconsulate, calculates, in his *De Mundi Duratione*, that the world will survive only another 101 years.[2]

This idea of an imminent death, closely bound moreover to the second coming of Christ, obsessed the entire first Christian generation.[3] Herein lies the unique example of a collective experience of death.[4] In the world of our experience, to realize this idea of death amounts to endowing our life with a new meaning. Actually, what is revealed here is the triumph of the flesh, of the physical terror before this appalling outcome. And it is no surprise that Christians have had such a bitter sense of the humiliation and anguish of the flesh and that these notions have been able to play a fundamental role in the development of Christian metaphysics. "My flesh is clothed with worms and dirt; my skin hardens, then breaks out afresh. My days are swifter than a weaver's shuttle, and come to their end without hope."[5] As we see it, the Old

---

1. P. de Labriolle, *La Réaction païenne*.

2. P. de Labriolle, *Histoire de la littérature latine chrétienne*.
[According to Labriolle, the title of Hilarianus's work is *De Mundi duratione* and not, as Camus says, *De Mundi induratione*. The page reference for this note, which is missing in Camus' text, is p. 402.—Trans.]

3. On the imminence of this parousia, cf. Mark 8:39–13:30; Matthew 10:23, 12:27–28, 24:34; Luke 9:26–27, 21:32. Cf also the Vulgate: Matthew 24:42–44, 25:13; Luke 12:37–40.

4. P. de Labriolle, *Histoire de la littérature*, p. 49: "Permeated with the sentiment that the world would soon die [one knows that this belief was common among the first Christian generations, but they appear to have felt it with a very particular intensity of anguish] they wanted . . ."

5. Job 7:5–6. [I have substituted the English translation of the Revised Standard Version in place of Camus' French translation of this text. All subsequent biblical passages cited by Camus will be taken from this translation.—Trans.]

Testament, with Job[6] and Ecclesiastes,[7] had already set the tone for this development.

But the Gospels have placed this sense of death at the center of their worship.

Actually, we are not sufficiently aware that Christianity is centered around the person of Christ and around his death. We turn Jesus into an abstraction or a symbol. But the true Christians are those who have realized the triumph of the martyred flesh. Jesus being fully human, the emphasis had been concentrated on his death, and one scarcely knows of a more physically horrible death.[8] It is on certain Catalonian sculptures, on the broken hands and the cracked joints, that one must reflect in order to imagine the terrifying image of torture that Christianity has erected as a symbol, but it suffices just as well to consult the well-known texts of the Gospel.

Another proof, if one is necessary, of the importance of this theme in Evangelical Christianity, is the indignation of the pagans. "Let her have her way with her empty illusions, and sing her sad, fond songs over her dead god who was condemned by the upright judges and, in his lonely years, met the ugliest death, linked with iron."[9] And again: "Why did he allow Himself to be mocked and crucified not saying anything worthy for the benefit of His judges or His hearers, but tolerating insults like the meanest of men."[10] But this is sufficient to prove the importance of

---

6. Job 2:9, 3:3, 10:8, 10:21–22, 12:23, 17:10–16, 21:23–26, 30:23.

7. *Passim*, but above all Ecclesiastes 2:17, 3:19–21, 12:1–8.

8. Cf. Renan, *Vie de Jésus*, ch. XXV, p. 438: "The particular atrocity of the punishment of the cross was that one could live three or four days in this horrible state. The haemorrhaging of the hands stopped and was not fatal. The true cause of death was the unnatural position of the body, which involved a frightful circulatory problem, terrible pains in the head and heart, and finally rigidity of the limbs."

9. Porphyry, *Philosophie des oracles*, according to Saint Augustine, *City of God*, XIX, 23: "Laisse-la donc, obstinée dans ses vaines erreurs, célébrer par de fausses lamentations, les funérailles de ce Dieu, mort, condamné par d'équitables juges et livré publiquement au plus ignominieux des supplices."

[Porphyry, *Philosophy of Oracles*, according to Saint Augustine, *City of God*, ed. V. J. Bourke, trans. G. Walsh, D. Zema, G. Monahan (New York: Image Books, 1958), 19.23, p. 472. Though Camus' reference suggests that Augustine is the direct source of this quotation, it seems that it is actually taken from P. de Labriolle, *La Réaction païenne*, p. 243, in which the passage is quoted in full, and which is the source of the following quotation from Porphyry. It should also be noted that in French, Camus can quote the sentence as if its subject were Christianity itself, while in English translation it unavoidably refers to Apollo's client's wife, who has embraced Christianity.—Trans.]

10. Porphyry, cited by P. de Labriolle, *La Réaction païenne*, p. 211 [*sic*]: "Il se laissa frapper, cracher au visage, couronner d'épines . . . même s'il devait souffrir par ordre de Dieu,

the sense of death and its flesh-and-blood contents in the thought that concerns us.

b) "We are laughable," says Pascal, "to remain in the company of our fellow men: miserable like us, powerless like us, they will not help us: one dies alone."[11] The experience of death carries with it a certain position that is tricky to define. There are actually numerous Gospel texts in which Jesus recommends indifference or even hatred toward one's loved ones as a way of reaching the Kingdom of God.[12] Is this the basis of an immoralism? No, but of a superior moral: "If any one comes to me and does not hate his own father and mother and wife and children and brothers and sisters, yes, and even his own life, he cannot be my disciple."[13] Through these texts we understand the extent to which the "Render unto Caesar" marks a contemptuous concession rather than a declaration of conformism. That which belongs to Caesar is the denarius on which is imprinted his effigy. That which belongs to God alone is man's heart, having severed all ties with the world. This is the mark of pessimism and not of acceptance. But as it is natural, these rather vague themes and these spiritual attitudes are made concrete and summed up in the specifically religious notion of sin.

c) In sin, man becomes aware of his misery and his pride. "No one is good;"[14] "All have sinned."[15] Sin is universal. But among all the significant[16] texts of the New Testament, few are as rich in meaning and insight

---

il aurait dû accepter le châtiment, mais ne pas endurer sa passion sans quelque discours hardi; quelque parole vigoureuse et sage, à l'adresse de Pilate, son juge, au lieu de se laisser insulter comme le premier venu de la canaille des carrefours."

[Porphyry, a fragment from his *Against the Christians,* trans. T. W. Crafer, in "The Work of Porphyry against the Christians, and Its Reconstruction," by T. W. Crafer, *Journal of Theological Studies* 15 (1913–1914): 502. Crafer's translation of these fragments from Porphyry's *Against the Christians* is, as far as I know, the only English translation available. In P. de Labriolle, Camus' source, the text is referred to as fragment no. 63. This system of enumeration is likely borrowed from Harnack, who first translated these texts. Crafer himself uses no standard form of enumeration. Though Crafer's translation of the text differs slightly, in terms of its detail, from Camus' French version, the meaning is clearly the same. The page reference from Labriolle should read p. 271.—Trans.]

11. [Camus does not offer a reference for this quotation from Pascal.—Trans.]

12. Matthew 8:22, 10:21–22 and 35–37, 12:46–50; Luke 3:34, 14:26–33.

13. Luke 14:26–28.

[The text should read: Luke 14:26.—Trans.]

14. ["Nemo bonus." Mark 10:18.—Trans.]

15. ["Omnes peccaverunt." Rom. 3:23.—Trans.]

16. John 1:8; 1 Corinthians 10:13; Matthew 12:21–23, 19:25–26.

as this passage from the Epistle to the Romans: "I do not understand my own actions. For I do not do what I want, but I do the very thing I hate. Now if I do what I do not want, I agree that the law is good . . . So I find it to be a law that when I want to do right, evil lies close at hand. For I delight in the law of God, in my inmost self, but I see in my members another law at war with the law of my mind and making me captive to the law of sin which dwells in my members."[17]

Here Saint Augustine's "incapacity not to sin"[18] becomes apparent. At the same time, the pessimistic soul of the Christians toward the world is explained. It is to this view and to these aspirations that the constructive element of Evangelical Christianity provides an answer. But it was useful to note beforehand this state of mind. "Let us imagine a number of men in chains and all condemned to death, of which some each day have their throats cut in the sight of the others, and those who remain see their true condition in that of their fellows, and, looking at each other with sorrow and hopelessness, await their turn. This is an image of man's condition."[19]

But in the same way that this Pascalian thought, situated at the beginning of the Apology, serves to emphasize the ultimate support for God, these men under the sentence of death are left with the hope that should have transported them.

B. *The Hope in God*

a) "Augustine: I desire to know God and the soul. Ratio: Nothing more? Augustine: Nothing whatever."[20] It is much the same in the Gospel, in which only the Kingdom of God counts, for the conquest of which one must renounce so much here below. The idea of the Kingdom of God is

---

17. Romans 7:15–24.
[The reference should read: Rom. 7:15–16, 22–23.—Trans.]
18. ["Non posse non peccare." Camus offers no reference for this passage. The text is from Saint Augustine's *De natura et gratia*, 57. The full sentence in which the remark occurs reads as follows: "Quia vero posse non peccare nostrum non est, et, si voluerimus non posse non peccare, non possumus non posse non peccare." "Inasmuch as, however, it is not of us to be able to avoid sin; even if we were to wish not to be able to avoid sin, it is not in our power to be unable to avoid sin." This translation is from www.ccel.org/fathers2/NPNF1–05/npnf1–05-16.htm#P2197_915376.—Trans.]
19. Pascal, *Pensées*, No. 199.
20. Saint Augustine, *Soliloquia*, I, 2, 7.
["Deum et animam scire Cupio," says Saint Augustine—"Nihil plus"—"Nihil omnino"

not absolutely new in the New Testament. The Jews already knew the word and the thing.[21] But in the Gospels, the Kingdom has nothing terrestrial about it.[22] It is spiritual. It is the contemplation of God himself. Apart from this conquest, no speculation is desirable. "I say this in order that no one may delude you with beguiling speech . . . See to it that no one makes a prey of you by philosophy and empty deceit, according to human tradition, according to the elemental spirits of the universe, and not according to Christ."[23] One must endeavor to attain the humility and simplicity of little children.[24] It is therefore to the children that the Kingdom of God is promised, but also to the learned who have known to divest themselves of their knowledge in order to understand the truth of the heart and who have added in this manner to this very virtue of simplicity the invaluable merit of their own effort. In *Octavius*,[25] Minucius Felix has Caecilius, defender of paganism, speak in these terms: "And thus all men must be indignant, all men must feel pain, that certain persons—and these unskilled in learning, strangers to literature, without knowledge even of sordid arts—should dare to determine on any certainty concerning the nature at large, and the (divine) majesty, of which so many of the multitude of sects in all ages (still doubt), and philosophy itself deliberates still." The explanation for this

[*sic*]. The text should read: "Augustinus: Deum et animam scire cupio. Ratio: Nihilne plus? Augustinus: Nihil omino." Augustine, *Soliloquiorum libri duo*, Opera Omnia, editio Latina, P.L. 32. www.augustinus.it/latino/soliloqui/index2.htm. The manner in which Camus cites the passage obscures its dramatic character as a dialogue between Augustine and his reason.—Trans.]

21. *Sagesse*, X, 10: "C'est celle qui conduisit par les voies droites le juste fuyant les colères de son frère; qui lui montra le royaume de Dieu et lui donna la science des choses saintes."

[The Wisdom of Solomon 10:10: "An upright man, who was a fugitive from a brother's wrath, she guided in straight paths; she showed him knowledge of holy things." In *The Apocrypha: An American Translation*, E. J. Goodspeed (New York: Random House, 1959), 196. The English translation lacks the reference to the Kingdom of God found in Camus' French translation.—Trans.]

22. Luke 12:14; Matthew 18:11, 20:28.

23. Colossians 2:18.

[The reference should read: Col. 2:4, 8.—Trans.]

24. Matthew 18:3, 4, and 19:16; Mark 10:14–15.

25. Minucius Felix, *Octavius*, VI, 4 [*sic*]: "Ne doit-on pas s'indigner que des gens qui n'ont pas étudié, étrangers aux lettres, inhabiles même dans les arts vils, émettent des opinions qu'ils tiennent pour certaines, sur tout ce qu'il y a de plus élevé et plus majestueux dans la nature, tandis que la philosophie en discute depuis des siècles?"

[Minucius Felix, *Octavius*, chap. 5, trans. R. E. Wallis, in *The Ante-Nicene Fathers*, ed. A. Roberts and J. Donaldson (1870; repr., Grand Rapids: Wm. B. Eerdmans, 1989), 4:175.—Trans.]

disdain for all pure speculation lies in the people who held emotional belief in God to be the goal of all human effort. But again a number of consequences follow from this view.

b) By placing man's striving toward God on the highest level, these Christians subordinate everything to this movement. The world itself is ordered according to the direction of this movement. The meaning of history is what God was willing to give it. The philosophy of history, a notion foreign to the Greek spirit, is a Jewish invention.[26] Metaphysical problems are incarnated in time, and the world becomes only a fleshly symbol of man's striving toward God. And here again, fundamental importance is given to faith.[27] It suffices that a paralytic or a blind man believes—this is what cures him. This is because the essence of faith is to consent and to relinquish. Moreover, faith is always more important than works.[28]

The reward in the next world retains a gratuitous character. It is of so high a price that it surpasses the requirement of merit. And here again, it is only a matter of an apology for humility. It is necessary to prefer the repentant sinner to the virtuous man, who is completely fulfilled in himself and in his good works. The laborer of the eleventh hour will be paid the same wage as those of the first hour. And a feast will be prepared for the prodigal child in his father's house. For the repentant sinner, there is eternal life. The word *eternal life* is taken, each time it is cited, in its broader meaning of immortality.[29]

c) Here then occurs the notion that interests us. If it is true that man is nothing and that his destiny is entirely in the hands of God, that works are not sufficient to assure him of his reward, if the "No one is good"[30] is well founded, who then will reach the Kingdom of God? The distance between God and man is so great that no one can hope to fill it. No man can reach God, and only despair is open to him. But then the Incarnation offers its solution. Man being unable to rejoin God, God descends to him. Thus is born the universal hope in Christ. Man was

---

26. [Camus makes the same argument about the Judaic origins of the philosophy of history in *The Rebel*: "In its idea of history, Christianity is Judaic and will be found again in German Ideology" (190).—Trans.]

27. Matthew 14:33, 12:58, 15:28.

28. Matthew 10:16–18, 20:1–16, 25:14–23.

29. Matthew 20:46, 25:34–36; Mark 10:17; Luke 10:24.

30. ["Nemo bonus."—Trans.]

right to put himself in God's hands, seeing that God offers him a most boundless grace.

It is in Paul that this doctrine is, for the first time, expressed in a coherent way.[31] For him, God's will has only one goal: to save man. Creation and redemption are only two manifestations of his will, the first and the second of his revelations.[32] The sin of Adam corrupted man and led to death.[33] He is left with no personal resources. The moral law of the Old Testament is content, in effect, to give man the image of the work he must achieve. But it does not give him the strength to achieve it. It thereby renders him twice guilty.[34] The only way for us to be saved had been for there to come to us, to release us from our sins by a miracle of grace, this Jesus, of our race, of our blood,[35] who represents us and is substituted for us. Dying with him and in him, man has paid for his sins: the Incarnation is at the same time redemption.[36] But for all that, the omnipotence of God is not reached, because the death and Incarnation of his son are graces and not sanctions owing to human merit.

This de facto solution resolved all the difficulties of a doctrine establishing such a great distance between man and God. Plato, who had wanted to unite the Good to man, had been constrained to construct an entire scale of ideas between these two terms. For that he created knowledge.[37] In Christianity, it is not reasoning that bridges this gap, but a fact: Jesus is come. To Greek wisdom, which is only a science, Christianity opposes itself as a state of affairs.

Finally, in order to understand fully the originality of a notion so familiar to us, we require the opinion of the pagans of the period. A spirit as cultivated as Celsus did not understand it. His indignation is real. Something escaped him which was far too new for him: "I turn now to consider an argument—made by Christians and some Jews—that some god or son of God has come down to earth as judge of mankind . . .

---

31. Colossians 1:15; 1 Corinthians 15:45; Romans 1:14.
32. Romans 1:20, 8:28; Ephesians 1:45, 3:11; 2 Timothy 1:9.
33. Romans 5:12, 14:15–17, 6:23.
34. Romans 3:20, 5:13, 7:7–8.
35. Romans 1:3, 4:4.
36. Romans 3:25, 6:6; 1 Corinthians 6:20; Galatians 3:13.
37. [Camus makes a similar claim in *The Rebel,* though there he does not identify Plato as its author: "Metaphysical rebellion presupposes a simplified view of creation—which was inconceivable to the Greeks. To their minds, there were not gods on the one side and men on the other, but a series of stages leading from one to the other" (28).—Trans.]

What is God's purpose in undertaking such a descent from the heights? Does he want to know what is going on among men? If he doesn't know, then he does not know everything. If he does know, why does he not simply correct men by his divine power? . . . Were they consistent, the Christians would argue that a god does not need to be known for his own sake, but rather wishes to give knowledge of himself for salvation— that is to say, in order to make people good and to distinguish the good from those who are bad and deserve punishment. But the Christian God is not so: he keeps his purposes to himself for ages, and watches with indifference as wickedness triumphs over good. Is it only after such a long time that God has remembered to judge the life of men?"[38] The Incarnation likewise seems unacceptable to Porphyry: "If the Greeks do think that the gods dwell in statues, at least it shows a purer mind than the belief that the deity went into the virgin's womb."[39] And Porphyry is astonished that Christ had been able to suffer on his cross, since he had to be by nature impassive.[40]

---

38. Celse, *Discours vrai,* Rougier trans., IV, 41: "Que si, dit-il, parmi les Chrétiens et les Juifs, il en est qui déclarent qu'un Dieu ou un fils de Dieu, les uns, doit descendre, les autres, soit descendu, c'est là de leur prétention la plus honteuse . . . Quel sens peut avoir pour un Dieu un voyage comme celui-là? Serait-ce pour apprendre ce qui se passe chez les hommes? Mais ne sait-il pas tout? Est-il donc incapable, étant donné sa puissance divine, de les améliorer sans dépêcher quelqu'un corporellement à cet effet . . . Et si, comme les chrétiens l'affirment, il est venu pour aider les hommes à rentrer dans la droite voie, pourquoi ne s'est-il avisé de ces devoirs qu'après les avoir laissés errer pendant tant de siècles."

[Celsus, *On the True Doctrine,* bk. 5, trans. R. J. Hoffmann (Oxford: Oxford University Press, 1987), 77. Because of the structure of the English translation of this text, a more lengthy portion had to be cited in order to communicate properly the meaning of Camus' French translation. It should also be noted that Camus' version of the text differs, though not significantly, from Rougier's translation. For the details of these differences, see Louis Rougier, *Celse contre les Chrétiens* (Paris: Copernic, 1977), 202. Rougier's book, chapter, and section numbering differ from Hoffmann's. Thus, apart from the omission of "bk. 2" from his note, Camus' reference is correct.—Trans.]

39. Porphyry, *Contre les Chrétiens,* fragment 77 in P. de Labriolle, *La Réaction païenne,* p. 274: "Même en supposant que tels des Grecs soient assez obtus pour penser que les Dieux habitent dans des statues, ce serait encore une conception plus pure que d'admettre que le Divin soit descendu dans le sein de la Vierge Marie, qu'il soit devenu embryon, qu'après sa naissance, il ait été enveloppé de langes, tout sali de sang, de bile et pis encore."

[Porphyry, fragment from *Against the Christians,* in Crafer, "The Work of Porphyry against the Christians," 506. The details offered in Camus' French text of Christ's descent into Mary's womb are missing from the English translation.—Trans.]

40. Ibid., fragment 84.

[The page reference for Camus' note is p. 274.—Trans.]

Nothing, therefore, is as specifically Christian as the notion of Incarnation. In it are summarized the obscure themes that we have tried to delimit. It is concerning this immediately comprehensible de facto argument, in which the movements of thought had their end, that it is necessary to observe it living in those it animated.

II. The Men of Evangelical Christianity

A. *The Works*

Distaste for speculation, practical and religious concerns, the primacy of faith, pessimism regarding man and the immense hope which is born of the Incarnation—so many of these themes come alive again in the first centuries of our era. Actually, one must be Greek in order to believe that wisdom is learned. Christian literature since its beginnings includes no moralist, right up to the time of Clement and Tertullian.[41] Saint Clement, Saint Ignatius, Saint Polycarp, the author of the doctrine of the twelve apostles and that of the apocryphal epistle, and the story of Barnabas are interested only in the religious side of problems. The apostolic story literature[42] is exclusively practical and popular. We must examine it in its details in order to form a fairly precise idea of its spirit and characteristics. This literature was developed from 50 to 90 CE. That is to say, it can claim to reflect the apostolic teaching. Be that as it may, it comprises the following: the first epistle of Saint Clement (93–97 CE), undoubtably written in Rome; the seven epistles of Saint Ignatius (107–117 CE), written in Antioch and along the coasts of Asia Minor; in Egypt, between 130 and 131 CE, the apocryphal Epistle of Barnabas;[43] *The Teaching of the Twelve Apostles,* probably written in Palestine (131–160 CE); the *Shepherd* of Hermas in Rome (140–155 CE); in Rome, or in

---

41. Tixeront, *Histoire des dogmes,* ch. III: "The Testimony of the Apostolic Fathers." [The full title of Tixeront's work is *Histoire des dogmes dans l'antiquité chrétienne.*— Trans.]

42. Ibid., chap. III, p. 115: "One gives the name of Apostolic Father to the ecclesiastic writers who appeared at the end of the first century or in the first half of the second century and who were supposed to have received from the apostles or their disciples immediately the instruction that they transmit to us."

43. Or *Didache.*

Corinth, the second epistle of Saint Clement in 150 CE; the fragments of Papias, in Hierapolis in Phrygia (150 CE); in Smyrna, the epistle of Saint Polycarp and his *Martyrium* (155–156 CE). But let us examine, rather, each of them and attempt to rediscover in them, in a pure state, the passionate postulates that we have already pointed out.

a) The sole aim the first epistle of Saint Clement sets for itself is to restore peace to the Corinthian Church. Its character is therefore purely practical. It insists upon the relation that exists between the leader of the Church and the Apostles, and then upon the relation between the latter and Jesus Christ, whose Incarnation saves us.[44] Wishing to subjugate the Corinthians to their spiritual leaders, he shows them that the cause of discord resides in envy, and he finds some pretext for speaking of humility and the virtue of obedience, which leads him to the praise of charity.[45] It is through humility that we obtain the forgiveness of our sins. Here can be found a second, specifically evangelical, point of view: those who are chosen are not chosen for their works but for their faith in God.[46] However, a little further on, Clement speaks of the need for works and of the inefficacy of faith without them.[47]

b) The letters of Saint Ignatius[48] are only topical writings, devoid of any methodological speculation. But Saint Ignatius is the one among the apostolic Fathers who had been most keenly aware of the Christ made flesh. He fights bitterly the docetic tendency in the bosom of Christianity. Jesus is "Son of God by the will and power of God; was really born of a virgin."[49] [He was the one] who "*in the flesh was of the line of David*, the Son of Man and the Son of God."[50] He affirms the real motherhood of Mary:

---

44. XXX, 6, in Tixeront, [*Histoire des dogmes,*] III, 2.

[The primary text to which this note refers is Saint Clement of Rome, *The Epistle to the Corinthians.*—Trans.]

45. Ibid., chap. XLIV.

46. Ibid., chap. XXXII, 3, 4.

47. Ibid., chap. XXXIII, 1.

48. For all that follows, cf. Tixeront, [*Histoire des Dogmes,*] ch. III, 5.

49. *Aux habitants de Smyrne*, I, 1: "Fils de Dieu suivant la volonté et la puissance de Dieu, fait vraiment d'une Vierge."

[Saint Ignatius, *The Epistle to the Smyrnaens*, 1.1, in *Ancient Christian Writers*, vol. 1, ed. J. Quasten and J. Plumpe, trans. J. A. Kleist (New York: Newman Press, 1946), 90.—Trans.]

50. *Ephesiens*, XX, 2 [*sic*]: "De la race de David selon la chair il est fils de l'homme et fils de Dieu."

[Saint Ignatius, *The Epistle to the Ephesians* 20.1, ibid., 68.—Trans.]

"truly born of a virgin."[51] "He had been truly pierced by a nail for us under Pontius Pilate and Herod the Tetrarch."[52] "And He suffered really, as He also really raised Himself from the dead. It is not as some unbelievers say, who maintain that His suffering was a make-believe."[53] Ignatius emphasizes still more, if it is possible, the humanity Christ has assumed. He maintains that it is in the flesh that Christ has risen. "I know and believe that He was in the flesh even after the Resurrection. And when He came to Peter and Peter's companions, He said to them: *'Here; feel me and see that I am not a bodiless ghost.'* Immediately they touched Him and, through this contact with His Flesh and Spirit, believed . . . Again, after the Resurrection, He ate and drank with them like a being of flesh and blood, though spiritually one with the Father."[54]

Upon this communion of Christ with us, Ignatius establishes the unity of the Church and the rules of religious life. For him, nothing is as valuable as Faith and Love. "Faith and love are paramount—the greatest blessings in the world."[55] And even carrying to the extreme one of the themes already indicated in primitive Christianity, he maintains that the one who has faith does not sin: "The carnal cannot live a spiritual life, nor can the spiritual live a carnal life, any more than faith can act the part of infidelity, or infidelity the part of faith. But even the things you do in the flesh are spiritual, for you do all things in union with Jesus Christ."[56] We have already defined this exalted type of Christianity,

---

51. *Eph.* VII, 2 [*sic*]: "Vraiment né d'une vierge."
[Saint Ignatius, *The Epistle to the Smyrnaeans,* 1.1, in *Ancient Christian Writers,* 90.—Trans.]
52. *Smyrne* I, 1, 2 [*sic*]: "Il a vraiment été percé de clous pour nous sous Ponce Pilate et Hérode le Tétrarque."
[Saint Ignatius, *The Epistle to the Smyrnaeans,* 1.2, ibid.—Trans.]
53. *Smyrne* II.
[Ibid., 90–91.—Trans.]
54. *Smyrne* III: "Je sais qu'après sa résurrection, Jesus a été en chair et je crois qu'il l'est encore. Et quand il vint à ceux qui étaient avec Pierre, il leur dit: 'Prenez, palpez-moi, et voyez que je ne suis pas un génie sans corps.' Et aussitôt ils le touchèrent et ils crurent, s'étant mêlés à sa chair et à son esprit . . . Et après la résurrection, il mangea et il but avec eux, comme étant corporel bien qu'étant uni spirituellement à son Père."
[Ibid., 91.—Trans.]
55. *Smyrne* VI, 1: "Le tout c'est la foi et la charité: il n'y a rien de plus précieux."
[Ibid., 92.—Trans.]
56. *Eph.,* 8, 2: "Les charnels ne peuvent faire les oeuvres spirituelles ni les spirituels les oeuvres de l'infidélité, ni l'infidélité celles de la foi. Les choses que vous faites selon la chair sont spirituelles, car vous faites tout en Jésus-Christ."
[Saint Ignatius, *The Epistle to the Ephesians,* 8.2, ibid., 63.—Trans.]

extreme in its faith and in the consequences that it presupposes: we will not be surprised, moreover, to find in Saint Ignatius the most passionate strains of mysticism. "My Love has been crucified, and I am not on fire with the love of earthly things. But there is in me a *Living Water,* which is eloquent and within me says: 'Come to the Father.'"[57]

c) The Epistle attributed to Saint Barnabas[58] is above all a polemical work directed against Judaism. It scarcely contains any doctrinal elements and moreover is of only mediocre interest. The author, with a great deal of realism, insists solely—and this is what should be noted—on Redemption. This Redemption derives from the fact that Jesus delivered up his flesh to destruction and sprinkled us with his blood.[59] Baptism is what allows us to participate in this Redemption. "We descend into the water, laden with sins and filth, and then emerge from it bearing fruit, with the fear (of God) in the heart and the hope of Jesus in the soul."[60]

d) "Two ways there are, one of life and one of death, and there is a great difference between the Two ways."[61] *The Teaching of the Twelve Apostles* is itself linked only to the teaching of what constitutes the path of life and of what must be done to avoid the path of death. It is a catechism, a liturgical formula, that does not contradict what we advanced about the exclusively practical character of all this literature.

e) The *Shepherd* of Hermas and the second epistle of Clement are above all works of edification.[62] The theme common to these two works is penance. Hermas accords penance solely to the faults committed at

57. *Rom.* VII, 2: "Mon amour est crucifié, et il n'y a point en moi de feu pour la matière; mais il y a une eau vive et parlante qui me dit intérieurement: 'Viens au Père'."

[Saint Ignatius, *The Epistle to the Romans,* 7.2, ibid., 83.—Trans.]

58. Tixeront, [*Histoire des Dogmes,*] ch. III, 8.

59. V, 1; VII, 3, 5.

[These are references to passages from the Epistle of Barnabas, as cited by Tixeront.—Trans.]

60. XI, XI, 1–8 [*sic*]: "Nous descendons dans l'eau, remplis de péchés et de souillures, et nous en sortons, portant des fruits, possédant dans le coeur et dans l'esprit, l'espérance en Jésus."

[The Epistle of Barnabas, 11.11, in *Ancient Christian Writers,* vol. 6, ed. J. Quasten and J. C. Plumpe, trans. J. A. Kleist (New York: Paulist Press, 1948), 54.—Trans.]

61. I, 1, in Tixeront, [*Histoire des Dogmes,*] ch. III, 8: "Il existe deux voies, l'une de la vie, l'autre de la mort, mais il y a une grande différence entre les deux."

[*The Teaching of the Twelve Apostles,* 1.1, ibid., 15.—Trans.]

62. Tixeront, [*Histoire des Dogmes,*] ch. III, 3 and 4.

the moment when he was writing. And from this moment the peniten-
tial doctrine is imbued with the particular rigor of pessimistic doctrines.
To the Christians of his time, he grants this penance only a single time.[63]
He establishes a rate according to which an hour of impious pleasure is
expiated by thirty days of penance, and a day by one year. According to
him, the wicked are doomed to flames, and whoever, knowing God, nevertheless committed evil, will atone for that sin eternally.[64]

The second epistle of Clement is a homily offering frequent analogies with the *Shepherd* of Hermas. Here again the aim is completely
practical: to exhort the faithful to Charity and Penitence. Chapters 1
through 9 demonstrate the real and tangible Incarnation of Jesus. The
following chapter is added to describe the punishments and rewards
that will be inflicted or accorded after the resurrection.

f) Polycarp's epistle, the relation to us which is made of his martyrdom, the fragments of Papias, finally, teach us nothing appreciably
new.[65] Dedicated to practical goals, these works join in an anti-docetic
Christology, a classical theory of sin, and the exaltation of Faith. They
actually summarize faithfully what we already know about this apostolic literature and its contempt for all speculation. Let us now inquire
into the milieu in which this preaching developed.

B. *The Men*

We can say that the apostolic Fathers' thought reflects the true face of
the period in which they lived. The first evangelical communities shared
these concerns and were withdrawn from all intellectual ambition.
Nothing better clarifies this state of mind than the efforts of Clement of
Alexandria to clear away these prejudices. If we consider that Clement
was living at the end of the second century,[66] we see with what tenacity

---

63. Manduc, IV, 3 [*sic*].

[Camus does not offer the name of the specific text he is citing, nor does any text by
Manduc appear in his bibliography. The reference seems to be to *Similitude* VI, chap. 3
of Hermas's *Shepherd*. See *The Ante-Nicene Fathers*, ed. Roberts and Donaldson (1870;
repr., Grand Rapids: Wm. B. Eerdmans, 1989), 2:7.—Trans.]

64. *Similit.* IV, 4 [*sic*].

[This reference should actually read: *Similitude* VI, chs. 4 and 5 of Hermas's *Shepherd*,
ibid., 37–38.—Trans.]

65. Tixeront, [*Histoire des Dogmes*,] ch. III, 6.

66. Between 180 and 203 CE.

Christianity clung to its origins, and all the more since the fantasies of Gnosticism were not meant to lead the spirit back toward philosophy.

Clement of Alexandria,[67] Greek in culture and in spirit, encountered the most lively resistance in his milieu, and all his efforts were to rehabilitate pagan philosophy, then in disrepute, and to accustom Christian spirits to it. But this is of another order. The *Stromateis* are of interest in that they reveal, through the author's resentment, that which was soundly hostile within his environment toward all speculation. Those whom Clement calls the *simpliciores* are indeed really the first Christians, and we find in them the postulates of apostolic preaching: "The multitude are frightened at the Hellenic philosophy, as children are at masks."[68] But the vexation makes itself felt: "Some, who think themselves naturally gifted, do not wish to touch either philosophy or logic, nay more, they do not wish to learn natural science."[69] Or again: "But to those who object, What use is there in knowing the causes of the manner of the sun's motion, for example, and the rest of the heavenly bodies, or in having studied the theorems of geometry or logic, and of each of the other branches of study?—for these are of no service in the discharge of duties, and the Hellenic philosophy is human wisdom, for it is incapable of teaching the truth—[the following remarks are to be made]."[70]

The opinions of the Christian milieu of Alexandria were perfectly clear. Faith suffices for man, and the rest is literature. Compare instead an assertion by Tertullian, a contemporary of Clement, to a text of the

---

67. De Faye, *Clément d'Alexandrie*, book II, ch. II.

68. *Stromates*, VII, 80 [*sic*]: "Le vulgaire a peur de la philosophie grecque comme les enfants ont peur d'un épouvantail."

[Clement of Alexandria, *Stromateis*, 7.10, trans. W. L. Alexander, in *The Ante-Nicene Fathers*, ed. Roberts and Donaldson (1870; repr., Grand Rapids: Wm. B. Eerdmans, 1989), 2:498.—Trans.]

69. *Stromates*, I, 43 [*sic*]: "Certaines gens qui se croient gens d'esprit estiment qu'on ne doit se mêler ni de philosophie, ni de dialectique, ni même s'appliquer à l'étude de l'univers."

[*Stromateis*, 1.9, ibid., 309.—Trans.]

70. Ibid., VI, 93 [*sic*]: "Il y a des personnes qui font cette objection. A quoi sert de savoir les causes qui expliquent le mouvement du soleil ou des autres astres ou d'avoir étudié la géométrie, la dialectique ou les autres sciences? Ces choses ne sont d'aucune utilité lorsqu'il s'agit de définir les devoirs. La philosophie grecque n'est qu'un produit de l'intelligence humaine: elle n'enseigne pas la vérité."

[*Stromateis*, 6.11, ibid., 501. The phrase in square brackets does not appear in Camus' French translation. It is necessary to add it in order to accommodate the syntax of the English translation.—Trans.]

latter, which confirm one another exactly. "What indeed has Athens to do with Jerusalem? What concord is there between the Academy and the Church? . . . Away with all attempts to produce a mottled Christianity of Stoic, Platonic, and dialectic composition! We want no curious disputation after possessing Christ Jesus, no inquisition after enjoying the gospel."[71] And Clement writes: "I am not oblivious of what is babbled by some, who in their ignorance are frightened at every noise, and say that we ought to occupy ourselves with what is most necessary, and which contains the faith, and that we should pass over what is beyond and superfluous."[72]

But these simple people limited themselves to the sacred Book. Saint Paul had put them on guard against "empty deceit."[73] Without charity, one could hope to be only the resounding bronze or the ringing cymbal. This is why in the fourth century, Rutilius Namatianus defined Christianity as the "sect that makes souls mindless."[74] And with that Clement of Alexandria is only vexed; Celsus is indignant.[75] This is certain proof of the vivacity of a tradition that he thus seems to us to have now established.

III. The Difficulties and Causes of Evangelical Christianity's Evolution

If we take a glance back, we must conclude that primitive Christianity is summarized in a few basic but inveterate themes, around which the

---

71. *De Prescriptione Haereticorum*, VII: "Qu'y a-t-il de commun, dit Tertullien, entre Athènes et Jérusalem, entre l'Académie et l'Eglise? . . . Tant pis pour ceux qui ont mis au jour un Christianisme stoïcien, platonicien, dialecticien. Pour nous, nous n'avons pas de curiosité après Jésus-Christ, ni de recherche après l'Evangile."
[Tertullian, *On Prescription against Heretics*, chap. 7, trans. P. Holmes, in *The Ante-Nicene Fathers* ed. Roberts and Donaldson (Edinburgh: T & T Clark, 1870), 15:9.—Trans.]
72. *Stromates*, I, 8 [sic]: "Je n'ignore pas ce que ressassent certaines gens ignorants qui s'effrayent du moindre bruit à savoir que l'on doit s'en tenir aux choses essentielles, à celles qui se rapportent à la foi, et que l'on doit négliger celles qui viennent du dehors et qui sont superflues."
[*Stromateis*, 1.1, trans. Alexander, in *The Ante-Nicene Fathers*, 2:303.—Trans.]
73. To the Colossians 2:8.
74. *De Reditu suo* I, 389, in Rougier, *Celse*, p. 112. "sect qui abêtit les âmes."*
[The reference should actually read: *De Reditu suo*, I, toward 398, in Rougier, *Celse contre les Chretiens*, 53.—Trans.]
75. *Discours vrai*, III, 37, trans. Rougier.

communities band together, full of these aspirations and attempting to embody them through their example and their preaching. These are the strong and bitter values that this new civilization implemented. Hence the excitement that accompanies its birth and the inner richness that it gives rise to in man.

But on these bases, an evolution is prepared. Already, from Matthew to John, its line of evolution comes to light. The Kingdom of God gives up its place to eternal life.[76] God is spirit, and it is in spirit that one must worship him. Christianity is already universalized. The Trinity, still undefined, is partially expressed nevertheless.[77] The point is that Christianity has already encountered the Greek world, and before going through some other forms of its evolution, it must check the causes that constantly push it to deepen itself and to spread its doctrines under the Greek mantle. The break with Judaism and entry into the Mediterranean spirit creates for Christianity some obligations: to satisfy the Greeks already accepted into the new religion, to entice the others to them by displaying a less Jewish Christianity and, in a general way, to speak their language, to express itself in understandable formulas and consequently to insert the uncoordinated enthusiasms of a profound faith into the handy forms of Greek thought. These are the necessities that we must clarify.

A. *The Adherents*

Since this period, in fact, and throughout the second century, Christianity counts among its adherents the most cultivated Greeks:[78] Aristides, whose *Apology to Antoninius the Pious* is placed between 136 and 161 CE; Miltiades (toward 150 CE); Justin, whose first *Apology* is situated between 150 and 155 CE, the second between 150 and 160 CE, and whose famous *Dialogue with Trypho* had been published toward 161 CE; Athenagoras, finally (*Supplicatio pro christianos* 176–178 CE)—

---

76. John 3:16, 36, and 4:14.
77. 5:19, 26.
[The reference should read: John, 5:19, 26.—Trans.]
78. Puech, *Les Apologistes grecs du IIe siècle.* In Tixeront, [*Histoire des Dogmes,*] 1.
[The full title of Puech's work is *Les Apologistes grecs du IIe siècle de notre ère.* Camus does not offer a page reference.—Trans.]

so many spirits who came to the new religion gave concrete expression to the union of a speculative tradition and a still-new sensibility in the Mediterranean basin.

From that moment on, it is a matter of them reconciling their spirit, which education had made Greek, and their heart, which Christian love had penetrated. Historically, these Fathers are apologists, because their whole effort is effectively to present Christianity as in harmony with Reason. Faith, according to them, completes the findings of Reason, and thus it is not shameful for a Greek spirit to accept it. It is therefore on philosophical ground that the two civilizations encountered one another.

Justin in particular comes a long way on this path. He relies on the similarities between Christian doctrine and Greek philosophy: the Gospel continues Plato and the Stoics.[79] And Justin sees two reasons for this coincidence. First, he accepted the idea, so widespread at the time,[80] that the Greek philosophers had knowledge of the Old Testament books and were inspired by them (a meaningless supposition, but one which had enormous popularity). Second, Justin thinks that the Logos itself appears to us in the person of Jesus, but that he existed before the Incarnation and inspired the philosophy of the Greeks.[81] This does not prevent our author from deciding in favor of the moral necessity of Revelation, because of the incomplete character of pagan speculation.

At the same time that the Apologists were drawing closer to the Greeks, they distanced themselves further and further from Judaism. The hostility of the Jews toward the new religion was sufficient ground. But it added a reason of political order, and this was the role the Jews had held in the persecutions by their accusations.[82] The entire argument of the *Dialogue with Trypho* is the demonstration of the agreement between the Prophets and the New Testament, from which Justin drew the prescriptions of the Old Testament and the triumph of Christian truth.[83]

79. *Apologie*, II, 13.
[The reference should read: Justin Martyr *Apologie* 2.13.—Trans.]
80. *Apologie*, I, 44, 59; Tatian, *Oratio ad Graecos*, 40; Minucius Felix, [*Octavius*,] 34; Tertullian, *Apologeticum*, 47; Clément d'Alexandrie, *Stromates*, I, 28; VI, 44; VI, 153; VI, 159.
81. Justin Martyr, *Apologie*, II, 13, 8, 10.
82. Justin Martyr, *Dialogue avec Tryphon* 16, 17, 108, 122, etc.; *Apologie*, I, 31–36.
[The English title of the former work is *Dialogue with Trypho*.—Trans.]
83. *Dialogue with Trypho*, 63 and *sq.*

B. *The Resistance*

At the same time, forms of resistance were also developing. We know, besides, of Tertullian's contempt regarding all pagan thought. Tatian[84] and Hermias[85] are also apostles of this particularist movement. But Christianity's most natural tendency is to extend itself, so the resistances of which we speak are those of the pagans. We can say without contradiction that these resistances contributed a great deal to the victory of Christianity. P. de Labriolle[86] strongly insists on the fact that the pagans at the end of the second century and at the beginning of the third apply themselves to diverting the religious enthusiasm of the period toward figures and personalities reproduced on the model of Christ.[87] This idea had already occurred to Celsus when he opposed Asclepius, Hercules, or Bacchus to Jesus. But this soon became a polemical system. At the beginning of the third century, Philostratus wrote the marvelous history of Apollonius of Tyana, which seems on many points to imitate the Scriptures.[88] Afterward, Socrates, Pythagoras, Hercules, Mithra, the sun, and the emperors would divert the favor of the Greco-Roman world and represent alternatively a pagan Christ. The method had its dangers and its advantages, but nothing better shows how well the Greeks had understood the strength and the appeal of the new religion. But this christianization of a decadent Hellenism also proves that the resistances were ingeniously made. And here again we see the necessity for Christianity to use its angles, to show to advantage its great dogmas on eternal life and the nature of God, and also to introduce in them metaphysics. That, in short, was the role of the Apologists. Moreover, they are not mistaken about it. This attempt at assimilation came from the highest levels. It goes back to Paul, born in Tarsus, a university and

---

84. *Oratio ad graecos* (165).
[*Address to the Greeks.*—Trans.]
85. *Irrisio gentilium philosophorum* (III\ufeffe siècle).
[*Mockery of the Heathen Philosophers.*—Trans.]
86. *La Réaction païenne*, second part, ch. II.
87. Cf. Boissier, *La Religion romaine*, preface, vol. I, IX: "Paganism tries to reform itself on the model of the religion that threatens it and which it combats."
[The title of Boissier's work is *La Fin du paganisme.*—Trans.]
88. Compare above all the episode of Ja'irus's daughter (Luke 7:40) and the *Vie d'Apollonius*, IV, 45 (p. 184 of Chassaing's translation).
[The reference to the story in Luke should read: Luke 8:40. The Latin title of the latter text is *Vita Apollonii,* or in English, *The Life of Apollonius.*—Trans.]

Hellenic city. In Philo it is particularly clear, but he takes a Jewish point of view. We have noted it in the Apologists alone because this is the first time in history that this movement assumes a coherent and collective form. Let us look only at the resulting problems.

C. *The Problems*

From this combination of evangelical faith with Greek metaphysics arose the Christian dogmas. Moreover, steeped in the atmosphere of religious tension, Greek philosophy gave rise to Neoplatonism.

But the thing was not made in a day. If it is true that the oppositions between Christian and Greek ideas were softened by the cosmopolitanism that we have noted, nevertheless some antinomies indeed remained; it was necessary to reconcile creation "ex nihilo," which excluded the hypothesis of matter, with the perfection of the Greek god, which implied the existence of this matter. The Greek spirit saw the difficulty of a perfect and immutable God creating the temporal and imperfect. As Saint Augustine wrote about this problem much later: "So then it is difficult to contemplate and have full knowledge of God's substance, which without any change in itself makes things that change, and without any passage of time in itself creates things that exist in time."[89] In other words, history made it necessary that Christianity deepen itself if it wanted to be universalized. This was to create a metaphysics. Now there is no metaphysics without a minimum of rationalism. Intelligence is powerless to renew its themes when sentiment endlessly varies its nuances. The effort of reconciliation inherent in Christianity will be to humanize and intellectualize its sentimental themes and to restore thought from these confines wherein it was struggling. This is because to explain is to a certain extent to have influence. This effort of reconciliation will therefore diminish slightly the disproportion between God and man that Christianity had established. It seems, on the contrary, that, in its beginnings, Christian thought, under the influence of the values of death and passion and the dread of sin

---

89. *De Trinitate*, I, 1, 3: "Il est difficile de comprendre la substance de Dieu qui fait des choses changeantes sans en éprouver aucun changement et des choses temporelles sans se mouvoir aucunement dans le Temps."

[Saint Augustine, *On the Trinity*, 1.1, 3, in *The Works of Saint Augustine*, vol. 5, ed. J. E. Rotelle, trans. E. Hill (Brooklyn: New City Press, 1991), 66.—Trans.]

and punishment, had arrived at the point where, as Hamlet says, time is out of joint. Intelligence must now give Christian thought its passage.

This was the task, in rather weak measure, of the first theological systems, those of Clement of Alexandria and Origen, as well as of the councils, in reaction against heresies, and above all of Saint Augustine. But, at precisely this point, Christian thought shifts. Christianity entered into a new phase in which it was a question of knowing whether it was losing its profound originality in order better to popularize itself, whether on the contrary it would sacrifice its power of expansion to its need for purity, or whether it would finally achieve a reconciliation of these equally natural concerns. But its evolution was not harmonious. It followed dangerous paths that taught it prudence. These were the paths of Gnosticism. Gnosticism made use of Neoplatonism and its convenient structures in order to accommodate religious thought. Permanently detached from Judaism, Christianity filtered into Hellenism through the door that Oriental religions were holding open. And upon that altar of the unknown God,[90] which Paul had encountered in Athens, several centuries of Christian speculation would be devoted to erecting the image of the Savior on the cross.

90. Acts 17:16.

Chapter Two

Gnosis

If we accept as an established fact this christianization of the Hellenic Mediterranean, we must consider the Gnostic heresy as one of the first attempts at Greco-Christian collaboration. Gnosticism is actually a Greek reflection upon Christian themes.[1] That is why it was repudiated both by the Greeks and by the Christians. Plotinus writes "against those who say that the . . . universe is evil."[2] And what Tertullian reproaches the Gnostics with in the *Adversus Marcionem* (as Saint Augustine did much later with the Manichaeans) is believing that they can attach to the Gospel a rational explanation. Nevertheless, it is true that the Gnostics were Christians. We find in them the theme of Incarnation. The problem of evil obsessed them. They have understood completely the originality of the New Testament and therefore of

1. [Camus offers a similar account of Gnosticism in his discussion of the origins of metaphysical rebellion in *The Rebel*, 32–33. The principal difference in that analysis lies in his assessment of the movement. In *The Rebel* Camus argues that Gnosticism was an essentially positive attempt to overcome the arbitrariness of the Christian idea of salvation by means of the Greek notion of initiation: "The Gnostics only wanted to substitute the Greek idea of initiation, which allows mankind every possible chance, for the concept of an all-powerful and arbitrary forgiveness" (33).]

2. Plotinus, *Ennead*, II, 9: "contre ceux qui disent que le monde est mauvais."

[This remark, which Camus indicates is taken from *Ennead* 2.9, is actually an alternative title of the text which Porphyry offers in his *Life of Plotinus*. The full title reads as follows: "Against those who say that the maker of the universe is evil and the universe is evil." See the introductory note of Plotinus, *Ennead*, 2.9, ed. T. E. Page, trans. A. H. Armstrong, Loeb Classical Library (Cambridge: Harvard University Press, 1964), 220.—Trans.]

Redemption. But rather than considering Christ made flesh and symbolizing suffering humanity, they incarnate only a mythology. When it comes to these authentic postulates of Christianity, the Gnostics devoted themselves to the subtle games of the Greek spirit. And upon the few simple and passionate aspirations of Christianity they build, as upon so many sturdy pillars, the whole setting of a metaphysical kermess. But a difficulty arises on this historical plane. The Gnostic schools follow one another for more than two centuries.[3] Several Gnostic generations have speculated in divergent directions. Valentinus and Basilides are spirits as different, relatively speaking, as Plato and Aristotle. How then are we to define Gnosticism? This is a difficulty that we have already encountered. If it is true that we can only define several gnosticisms, it is possible nevertheless to characterize one gnosis. The first Gnostic generation,[4] that of Basilides, Marcion, and Valentinus, created the web upon which their disciples embroidered. A small number of common themes will be sufficient in order to catch a glimpse of this heretical solution. Historically, in fact, Gnosticism is a philosophical and religious instruction, given to the initiated, based upon Christian dogmas mingled with pagan philosophy, which assimilated all that was splendid and brilliant in the most diverse religions.

But before indicating the themes of the Gnostic solution and revealing its origins, it is necessary to see how it fits into the movement of thought being considered in this work. This is, moreover, to redefine gnosis, this time on the metaphysical plane. Gnosticism poses problems in a Christian manner. It solves them in Greek formulas. Basilides and Marcion are actually persuaded of the wretchedness of the world. But insofar as one accuses the carnal side of reality, one expands the catalogue of sins and wretchedness and increasingly widens the gulf between man and God. There will come a time when no repenting nor any sacrifice will suffice to fill in such a chasm. It suffices to know God to be saved.[5] Otherwise, any works or any other source would be able to draw man out of his nothingness. This is, as we have seen, the Christian solution of salvation through Incarnation. It is also, in one

---

3. From the beginning of the second century to the end of the third.
4. The first half of the second century.
5. Cf. in Buddhism, the parent form of Amitabha.

sense, the solution of the Gnostics. But Christian grace retains a character of divine arbitrariness. The Gnostics, unaware of the profound meaning of the Incarnation, restricting it in its significance, have transformed the notion of salvation into that of initiation. Valentinus actually separated humanity into three orders or types:[6] materialists, who are tied to the goods of this world; psychics, balanced between God and matter; and the spiritual, who alone live in God and know him. The latter are saved as later will be the Chosen ones of Mani. Here is introduced the Greek notion. The spiritual are saved only by gnosis or knowledge of God. But this gnosis they learn from Valentinus and from men. Salvation is learned. It is therefore an initiation. For though these notions of salvation and initiation appear, at first sight, related, analysis can no doubt discern subtle but fundamental differences between them. Initiation gives man influence over the divine kingdom. Salvation admits him to this kingdom, without his having any part in achieving it. One can believe in God without being saved. It was sufficient to contemplate the mysteries of Eleusis.[7] On the other hand, baptism does not imply salvation. Hellenism cannot be separated from this hope, about which it is so tenacious, that man holds his destiny in his own hands. And at the very heart of Christianity there was, as it happens, a tendency slowly to draw the notion of salvation back into that of initiation. In the same way that the Egyptian fellah slowly won, through the Pharaoh, the right to immortality, the Christian, through the Church, finally had in his hands the keys to the kingdom of heaven.

It is quite right, one sees, that we are able to consider Gnosticism as one of the solutions, one of the Christian stages in the problem that we detect: gnosis is an attempt to reconcile knowledge and salvation. But let us now look at the detail of this attempt.

---

6. De Faye, *Gnostiques et Gnosticisme*, I, ch. II. Amelineau, *Essai sur le Gnosticisme égyptien*.

7. Cf. *Hymne homérique à Déméter*, 480–83: "Heureux, celui des hommes vivant sur la terre qui a vu ces choses. Mais celui qui n'a pas été initié aux cérémonies sacrées et celui qui y a pris part n'auront jamais la même destinée après la mort dans les vastes ténèbres." P. Loisy, [*Les mystères païens et le mystère chrétien,*] p. 76.

[*Homeric Hymn to Demeter*, 480–83: "Happy are those men living on earth who have seen these things. But those who have not been initiated into the sacred ceremonies and those have taken part will never have the same destiny after death in the vast darkness."*]

I. The Themes of the Gnostic Solution

More or less emphasized in the different authors, four fundamental themes are found at the heart of the entire Gnostic system: the problem of evil, redemption, the theory of intermediaries, and a conception of God as an ineffable and incommunicable being.

a) If it is true that the problem of evil had been at the center of all Christian thought, no one had been more profoundly Christian than Basilides.

This original figure is not very widely known. We know that he lived under the reigns of Hadrian and Antoninus the Pious (that is to say, toward 140 CE) and that he probably began to write toward 80 CE. The only partially complete note on his thought is now considered as having little foundation. This note is one of the *Philosophumena,* which in all likelihood deals with a pseudo-Basilides. Our most important source remains Clement of Alexandria, in his *Stromateis.* Irenaeus speaks of Basilides in his catalogue, Epiphanius in his *Contra Haereses* (chapter 24). Finally, we can put together a few allusions from Origen.[8]

"The origin of this evil doctrine is in the inquiry about where evil is from."[9] This is, in fact, what stands out from the little we know of Basilidean thought. Removed from all speculation, he devoted himself only to moral problems, and more precisely to that moral problem which was born of the relations between man and God. What interests him is sin and the human side of the problem. From faith itself he creates a natural and real existence. "Basilides seems incapable of conceiving an abstraction. It is necessary for him to give it an appearance of substance."[10]

It is from this point of view that Basilides develops his thought and is bound to establish a theory of original sin. To tell the truth, the word does not exist in his thought, but only the idea of a certain natural predisposition to sin. Finally, he adds two complementary assertions: sin

8. *Commentary on Romans* V; *Homily on Luke* I; *Commentary on Matthew* 38.

9. *Contra Haereses,* XXIV, 6, 72c [*sic*]: "L'origine et la cause de cette mauvaise doctrine, dit Épiphane, c'est la recherche et la discussion du problème du Mal."

[Epiphanius, *Panarion,* 24.6.1, in *The Panarion of St. Epiphanius, Bishop of Salamis: Selected Passages,* ed. and trans. P. R. Amidon (Oxford: Oxford University Press, 1990), 70.—Trans.]

10. De Faye, [*Gnostiques et Gnosticisme,*] 31.

always carries with it a punishment, and there is always an enrichment and an atonement to draw out of suffering. These three themes are attributed indiscriminately to Basilides and to his son, Isidore.

Be that as it may, Basilides is deeply struck by the fate of martyrs. According to him, martyrdom is not useless suffering. Each suffering requires a previous sin that justifies it. Basilides must therefore conclude that martyrs have sinned. Moreover, this state is perfectly reconciled with their holiness. It is precisely their privilege to be able to atone so completely for their past. But who is the greatest of the martyrs, if not Jesus himself? "If you were to insist more urgently, I would say, That the man you name is a man, but that God is righteous. 'For no one is pure,' as one said, 'from pollution.'"[11] The allusion is transparent, and we understand why the doctrine was viewed unfavorably by Epiphanius. Christ does not escape the universal law of sin. But at least he shows us the path of deliverance, which is the cross. This is why Basilides and his son, Isidore, inaugurated, to a certain extent, an ascetic life.[12] Moreover, it was necessary for Isidore, because it is to him that we owe the theory of the appendage passions. The passions do not belong to us but cling to the soul and exploit us.

Isidore saw clearly that a similar theory could lead the wicked to present themselves as victims and not as guilty. Hence, the ascetic rule of life.

This is what remains for us of Basilides' philosophy. We scarcely see how these few reports could be in harmony with the instructions of Hippolytus in the *Philosophumena*.[13] According to Hippolytus, Basilides would have conceived the idea of an abstract God, residing in the ogdoad, separated from our world by the intermediary universe, or hebdomad. The God of this intermediary world, the great Archon, Basilides would have identified with the God of the Old Testament: "The Ogdoad

11. Cited by De Faye, ch. I: "Si l'on me pousse, je dirai qu'un homme, quel que soit celui que tu nommes, est toujours homme, tandis que Dieu est juste. Car comme on l'a dit, personne n'est pur de toute souilure."

[Clement of Alexandria, *Stromateis*, trans. W. L. Alexander, in *The Ante-Nicene Fathers*, ed. A. Roberts and J. Donaldson (1870; repr., Grand Rapids: Wm. B. Eerdmans, 1989), 2:424. De Faye himself offers no reference for this text. It is, as I have indicated, from Clement's *Stromateis*. The passage is found on p. 42 in De Faye.—Trans.]

12. Cf. De Faye, [*Gnostiques et Gnosticisme*,] ch. I, 26–27.

13. Hippolytus, *Philosophumena*, bk. VII [*sic*].

[The more common English title of this work is *The Refutation of All Heresies*.—Trans.]

is Arrhetus, whereas the Hebdomad is Rhetus. This, he says, is the Archon of the Hebdomad, who has spoken to Moses, and says: 'I am the God of Abraham, and Isaac and Jacob, and I have not manifested unto them the name of God,' (for so they wished it had been written)—that is, the God, Arrhetus, Archon of the Ogdoad."[14]

This metaphysical cosmology does not seem very compatible with the profound tendencies of our author, above all when we attribute to him a) the idea that Christ did not die crucified, but that he took the place of Simon of Cyrene, b) and the grandiose eschatology that predicts the following: "When this takes place, God . . . will bring upon the whole world enormous ignorance, that all things may continue according to nature, and that nothing may inordinately desire any of the things that are contrary to nature."[15] This is the center of Basilides' meditations: it is the problem of evil and, to speak anachronistically, of predestination. The earlier doctrines are far too developed: we would say decadent. One single affirmation of Hippolytus might make us doubt. This is when he attributes to his author the idea that the soul has no more freedom of action than the freedom of belief. It is by nature inclined to sin and will inevitably fail.

We will have to grasp the importance of the problem of evil in the writings of the Gnostic least known to us. It is the same in all Gnostic sects.[16] We will not be surprised, therefore, to find, placed in the same standing, the closely related problem of Redemption.

b) Marcion[17] is the one among the Gnostics who was most keenly aware of the originality of Christianity. He was aware to such a point that he turned contempt for the Jewish law into a moral. Marcion is not

---

14. Ibid., VII, p. 125 [*sic*], in Amelineau, [*Essai sur le Gnosticisme égyptien,*] II, 2.

[Hippolytus, *The Refutation of All Heresies,* 7.13, trans. J. H. MacMahon, in *The Ante-Nicene Fathers,* ed. A. Roberts and J. Donaldson (1870; repr., Grand Rapids: Wm. B. Eerdmans, 1989), 5:106.—Trans.]

15. Cited by Amelineau, p. 135 [*sic*]: "Quand tout cela sera définitivement accompli, quand toutes les formes confondues auront été dégagées, et rendues à leur place primitive, Dieu répandra une ignorance absolue sur le monde entier afin que tous les êtres qui le composent restent dans les limites de leur nature et qu'ils ne désirent rien qui en soit en dehors." Compare this with the old Egyptian beliefs: "The rebels will become motionless during the millions of years." Cited by Amelineau, p. 152.*

[Hippolytus, *The Refutation of All Heresies,* 7.15, ibid., 108.—Trans.]

16. De Faye, [*Gnostiques et Gnosticisme,*] in his conclusion, pp. 460–63.

17. In Tertullian, *Adversus Marcionem;* Clement of Alexandria, *Stromates;* Origen, *De Principiis,* bk. II, chs. IV and V; and Philaster, *Epiphane pseudo Tertullien;* Irenaeus.

a speculative thinker but a religious genius. We do not discover in him a system similar to the one of Valentinus. He has founded neither a church nor a school; his books are not original but exegetical.[18] In a general way, his thought revolves around three points: first, God; second, Redemption and the person of Christ; and third, morality.

There are two divinities for Marcion: the one is superior and rules in the invisible world, the other is subordinate and is the God of this world. "Well, but our god . . . although he did not manifest himself from the beginnings and by means of the creation, has yet revealed himself in Christ Jesus."[19] The God of creation is the second God, the cruel and warlike judge, the God of the Old Testament, the one who persecuted Job to prove his power to Satan, who demanded blood and battles and whose law oppressed the Jewish people.[20] There is no Avestic influence here. It is not a matter of two opposing principles of equal force whose struggle sustains the world, but of a God and a demiurge between whom the fight is unequal. By stating the problem in this way, Marcion claimed to be in the truth and could rely on the Gospels (or rather, on the only Gospel he acknowledged, the Gospel of Luke): "No one tears a piece from a new garment and puts it upon an old garment . . . And no one puts new wine into old wine skins."[21] And again: "No good tree bears bad fruit, nor again does a bad tree bear good fruit."[22] Above all, he commented on the Epistle

18. De Faye, [*Gnostiques et Gnosticisme,*] I, 4.

19. In *Adversus Marcionem*, ch. VIII [*sic*]: "Notre Dieu n'a pas été révélé dès le commencement, il ne l'a pas été par la création; il s'est révélé lui-même en Jésus-Christ." Cf. also *Adversus Marcionem* I, 16: "Consequens est ut duas species rerum visibilia et invisibilia duobus auctoribus deis dividant et ita suo deo invisibilia defendant," and L, XVII, I, 6. [The first passage cited is from Tertullian, *Against Marcion*, 1.19, trans. P. Holmes, in *The Ante-Nicene Fathers*, ed. A. Roberts and J. Donaldson (1870; repr., Grand Rapids: Wm. B. Eerdmans, 1989), 3:284. The second text, quoted in Latin, is from Tertullian, *Against Marcion*, 1.16, ibid., 282: "The only resource left to them is to divide things into two classes of visible and invisible, with two gods for their authors, and so to claim the invisible for their own, (the supreme) God."—Trans.]

20. [There is a remarkably similar assessment of the Jewish God in *The Rebel:* "Until Dostoievsky and Nietzsche, rebellion is directed only against a cruel and capricious divinity—a divinity who prefers, without any convincing motive, Abel's sacrifice to Cain's, and by so doing, provokes the first murder." Camus says that in this regard "it is the God of the Old Testament who is primarily responsible for mobilizing the forces of rebellion (32–33).—Trans.]

21. Luke 5:36. [The reference should read: Luke 5:36–37.—Trans.]

22. Luke 6:43.

to the Galatians. And in the continual contrast that Paul makes between the Law and the Gospel, Judaism and Christianity, Marcion believed he saw proof that the two Testaments were inspired by different authors. In the writings of Valentinus also we find this idea of a creator different from the one God. But for him it is a matter of a logical solution necessitated by the problem of evil. With Marcion, on the contrary, it is the very keen sense of the novelty of Christianity that gave birth to this radical opposition. In this sense, we have been right to speak of a political[23] rather than a metaphysical thought in the work of Marcion.

We see already the importance that Christ will take on for Marcion. He is nothing less than the envoy of the supreme God, sent to combat the wicked God, the creator of the world, and to deliver man from his domination. Jesus accomplished here below a revolutionary mission. If he atoned for our sins, it is through them that he combats the work of the cruel God. Emancipator as much as Redeemer, he is the instrument of a kind of metaphysical coup d'etat. "Marcion has laid down the position, that Christ who in the days of Tiberius was, by a previously unknown god, revealed for the salvation of all nations, is a different being from Him who was ordained by God for the restoration of the Jewish state, and who is yet to come. Between these he interposes the separation of a great and absolute difference—as great as lies between what is just and what is good; as great as between the law and the gospel; as great, (in short) as is the difference between Judaism and Christianity."[24] In support of this remarkable theory, Marcion cites a number of texts, which he interprets in his own way and which he draws mostly from Luke's Gospel. "What father among you, if his son asks for a fish, will instead of a fish give him a serpent? . . . If you then, who are evil, know how to give good gifts to your children, how much more will the heavenly Father give the Holy Spirit to those who ask him!"[25] This

---

23. De Faye, [*Gnostiques et Gnosticisme,*] p. 130.

24. Tertullian, *Adversus Marcionem*, IV, 6: "Marcion prétend qu'il y a deux Christs; l'un est révélé au temps de Tibère par un Dieu que l'on ne connaissait pas, avec mission de sauver tous les peuples; l'autre était destiné par le Dieu créateur à restaurer Israël et devait apparaître un jour. Il fait entre ces deux Christs autant de différence qu'entre la Loi et L'Évangile, le Judaïsme et le Christianisme."

[Tertullian, *Against Marcion*, 4.6, trans. Holmes, in *The Ante-Nicene Fathers*, 3:351.—Trans.]

25. Luke 5:12–14, 5:27–32, 7:9–10, [chs.] 11 and 16, 18:19.

[This list of references seems to indicate those texts from Luke on which Marcion bases his theory. The text that Camus actually quotes is from Luke 11:11, 13.—Trans.]

strange interpretation finds its crowning achievement in morality. The rule of life that Marcion proposes is ascetic. But it is a proud or arrogant asceticism. One must scorn the goods of this world out of hatred for the Creator. One must give as little influence as possible to his domination. This is Marcion's ideal. It is a most extreme asceticism. And if Marcion preaches sexual abstinence, it is because the God of the Old Testament says: "Increase and multiply." In this pessimistic view of the world and this proud refusal to accept can be found the resonance of a completely modern sensibility. This pessimistic view also has its source in the problem of evil. Marcion considers the world to be wicked but refuses to believe that God can be its author. If his solution revolves around Redemption, it is because he views the role of Christ in a more ambitious manner than the Christians themselves. It is a matter of nothing less than the complete destruction of creation.

c) The last two themes of Gnosticism must be considered as closely linked. For if one makes God an incommunicable and nontemporal being, one does not, for all that, give up supposing in him an interest in the world. It is necessary, then, to explain these relations between God and man and, not being able to bring into contact this nothingness and this infinite, at least to acknowledge one or more intermediaries participating at once in the divine infinity and in our finitude. To find these middle terms is more or less the great problem of the first centuries of our era. The Gnostics have not at all lacked such intermediaries to follow. They even provide for their production a luxury and an unequaled splendor.

The first Gnostic generation was content to consider God as ineffable and inexpressible. But at least they believed in him firmly. Their successors went even further, and certain of their expressions often remind one of the Brahman of the *Upanishads,* who can only be defined by "not not." "(Time) was, says (Basilides), when there was nothing. Not even, however, did that nothing constitute anything of existent things; but, to express myself undisguisedly and candidly, without any quibbling, it is altogether nothing. But when, he says, I employ the expression 'was,' I do not say that it was; but (I speak this way) in order to signify the meaning of what I wish to elucidate."[26] And again: "He who speaks the word

---

26. *Philosophumena* I, VII, p. 20 [*sic*]: "Ce Dieu, dit le pseudo-Basilide, était lorsque le rien était, mais ce rien n'était pas quelqu'une des choses qui existent maintenant, et, pour parler ouvertement, simplement et sans subtilité, seul le rien existait. Or, quand je

. . . was non-existent; nor was that existent which was being produced. The seed of the cosmical system was generated . . . from nonentities; (and I mean by the seed,) the word which was spoken, 'Let there be light.' And this . . . is that which has been stated in the Gospels: 'He was the true light, which lighteth every man that cometh into the world.'"[27] Hippolytus summarizes these remarks as follows: "In this way, 'nonexistent' God made the world out of nonentities, casting and depositing some one Seed that contained in itself a conglomeration of the germs of the world."[28] But one must take into account Hippolytus's sentiments and realize that this excessive subtlety is not the rule with the Gnostics. On the contrary, it seems that Valentinus had had a very keen sense of the divine nature. It is only in the doctrine of intermediaries that he gave free reign to his imagination.

d) Valentinus is the Gnostic whose work we know the best.[29] On the other hand, about his life we have no information, to such an extent that some have cast doubt on his very existence. His very coherent system can be divided into a theology, a cosmology, and a morality. It is the most curious example of this incarnation of mythology of which we spoke earlier. To tell the truth, the pleroma that Valentinus places between God and the earth is a Christian Olympus. At least it is Christian in intention, but in form and imagination it is Greek. Valentinus's philosophy is a metaphysics in action, a tremendous tragedy that is played out in heaven and earth, and in the infinity of Time, a struggle of problems and symbols, something like the *Roman de la Rose* of Gnostic thought.

---

dis qu'il existait, je ne veux pas dire qu'il a réellement existé, je veux seulement montrer ma pensée."

[Hippolytus, *The Refutation of All Heresies*, 7.8, trans. MacMahon, in *The Ante-Nicene Fathers*, 5:103. The reader should note that in MacMahon's translation, the subject of this passage is Time, and not God, as it is in Camus' French text.—Trans.]

27. *Philosophumena*, 340, lines 12–15 [*sic*]: "Celui qui parlait n'existait pas, et ce qui fut ensuite créé n'était pas davantage; donc de ce qui n'était pas fut fait le germe du monde, c'est-à-dire cette parole qui fut prononcée par le Dieu néant: Que la lumière soit; et c'est ce qui est écrit dans l'Évangile. Il est la lumière illuminant tout homme venant en ce monde."

[Hippolytus, *The Refutation of All Heresies*, 7.10, ibid., 104.—Trans.]

28. *Philosophumena*, VII, 22 [*sic*]: "Ainsi Dieu non existant a afit un cosmos non existant d'éléments non existants en émettant un germe unique qui contenait tous les germes du cosmos."

[Hippolytus, *The Refutation of All Heresies*, 7.9, ibid.—Trans.]

29. *Philosophumena* and *Stromates*, XIII.

1) Valentinus's God[30] is uncreated and timeless. But solitary and perfect, he superabounds as a result of his perfection. By thus superabounding he created a Dyad, one of Spirit and Truth. This pair in its turn generates Word and Life, which produce Anthropos and Ecclesia. From these six principles now arise the pleroma intact, which is composed of two groups of angels, or æons, the one containing a dozen, the other containing ten, that is to say, in Gnostic terms, the decade and the dodecade.[31] Spirit and Truth, wanting to glorify the divinity, create a chorus of ten æons whose mission is to render homage to God. They are created in the following order: the Abyss, the Mixed, the One who is ageless, Unity, the One who is of his own nature, Pleasure, the One who is motionless, the Mixture, the only Son, and Happiness. Word and Life in their turn—but this time with the goal of glorifying the active Spirit—create the dodecade. The dodecade is composed of the dozen eons prepared in syzygies, that is to say, in pairs of male and female. They are: the Paraclete and Faith, the Father and Hope, the Mother and Love, Prudence and Intelligence, the Ecclesiastic and the Very Happy, the Volunteer and Wisdom. Together these æons form the pleroma, midway between God and the world. But what the world is and its relation to this theology and æonology Valentinus is going to teach us.

2) It is remarkable that thus far God alone has created without the help of a female principle. He alone is perfect. He alone superabounds. It is through their union that Spirit and Truth or Word and Life succeeded in generating, respectively, the decade and the dodecade. Now the last born of the eons, Sophia, or Wisdom, from the bottom of the ladder of principles, turned around and wanted to see God.[32] In this manner, she knew that God alone had created. Through pride and envy, she attempted to create on her own. But she succeeds in creating only one formless being, of which it is said in Genesis: "The earth was without form and void."[33] Sophia then recognized with great sorrow her ignorance and, full of fear, was moved to despair. These four passions constitute the four elements of the world. And Sophia lives forever joined to this formless fetus she

---

30. De Faye, [*Gnostiques et Gnosticisme,*] I, 2. Amelineau, [*Essai sur le Gnosticisme égyptien,*] III, 1, 2, 3, 4, 5.

31. The dodecade is devoted to the active Spirit; the decade, a perfect number according to the Pythagoreans, is devoted to a perfect God.

32. De Faye, [*Gnostiques et Gnosticisme,*] ch. II.

33. Genesis 1:2.

had created. But God took pity on her and again created a special principle, the principle of Horos,[34] or Limit. Limit, coming to the aid of
Sophia, will restore her to her original nature and cast the world out of
the pleroma, thus reestablishing the original harmony. At this moment
a demiurge intervenes, and arranging matter, makes from it the cosmos.
Utilizing Sophia's passion, he created men. These men are divided into
three categories according to the level of consciousness of their origin:[35]
the spiritual, who aspire to God; the materialists, who have no memory
and therefore no concern for their origins; and between the two, the psychics, the indecisive, who run from the vulgar life of the senses to the
most elevated anxieties without knowing which to hold on to. But they
all bear the mark of their birth: they have been born of fear, ignorance,
and sorrow. Hence the need for Redemption. But it is the Spirit this time
who, transforming himself into Christ, came to deliver man from his ill-
fated seed. Things are further complicated when we learn that the
Redeemer was not Jesus. Jesus is born of the acknowledgment of the eons
regarding the God who had reestablished order. They therefore gather
their virtues and offer to God in thanksgiving the being thus formed.
Redemption, on the contrary, is a work of the Holy Spirit who has
revealed to men their divine part and who has brought about in them
the death of their sinful part. This is without doubt the meaning of that
enigmatic text of the *Stromateis:* "'Ye are originally mortal, and children
of eternal life, and ye would have death distributed to you, that ye may
spend and lavish it, and that death may die in you and by you; for when
we dissolve the world, and are not yourselves dissolved, ye have domin-
ion over all creation and all corruption.'"[36]

3) Valentinus's ethic is closely tied to his cosmology. For all that, his
cosmology is only a solution adapted to a problem that obsessed him,
the problem of evil. "I came to believe in the reality that tragedies

---

34. Cf. De Faye, [*Gnostiques et Gnosticisme,*] p. 238.
35. Cf. Amelineau, [*Essai sur le Gnosticisme égyptien,*] p. 219. De Faye, [*Gnostiques et Gnosticisme,*] p. 45.
36. *Stromates,* XIII, 85, according to De Faye, [*Clément d'Alexandrie,*] p. 42: "Vous êtes immortels depuis le commencement; vous êtes enfants de la vie éternelle et vous voulez partager la mort afin que vous la dépensiez et l'épuisiez et que la mort meure en vous et par vous. Car lorsque vous désagrégez le monde et que vous-mêmes n'êtes pas désagrégés, vous êtes maîtres de la création et de la corruption tout entière."
[Clement of Alexandria, *Stromateis,* 13, trans. Alexander, in *The Ante-Nicene Fathers,* 2:425.—Trans.].

represented, I am persuaded that they only place the truth before our eyes. I believe in Oenomaüs' desire during his intoxication, I do not regard as an unbelievable thing that two brothers may have been able to fight one another. And I could not find the strength within me to say that God was the author and creator of all this evil."[37] It is therefore the problem of evil that directed Valentinus toward these speculations. And the conclusion he draws from his cosmology is very simple: there is no freedom in the human soul as a result of Sophia's error. Only those who regain an awareness of their origins will be saved, that is to say, the Gnostics and the spiritual. Salvation is contemporaneous with knowledge. As for the psychics, they can be saved, but it is necessary that they put themselves in the hands of the divine arbitrariness.

It is here that Valentinus's thought rejoins the common foundation of all Gnostics. But, in his turn, his æonology and cosmology must have known a very great success in the throng of small schools in which Gnosticism came to an end and which remain for us to characterize briefly in order to complete our study of Gnosticism.

If we adopt the classification that seems most well-informed, that of M. de Faye, the themes that we have just covered are found in three groups of schools: a group studied by the heresiologists and which we can call the Followers of the Mother; next, and through the medium of the previous ones, these themes are passed on to the Gnostics, the majority of which are mentioned in the *Philosophumena,* and to a group of Coptic Gnostics of whom the *Codex Brucianus* and the *Pistis Sophia* give us a faithful image. Moreover, the relation between them is completely theoretical, because, if it is true that the Followers of the Mother roughly preceded in time the two later groups, each of the three schools is composed of such a large number of sects that it is likely that they overlapped each other and that they have intertwined their themes. But the intellectual relation is real, just as the necessities of exposition render this classification indispensable. We will limit ourselves, moreover,

---

37. Cited by the author of the *Dialogue contre les Marcionites,* Amelineau, [*Essai sur le Gnosticisme égyptien,*] p. 230: "J'en vins à croire à la réalité de ce qu'ont représenté les tragédies, je suis persuadé qu'elles ne mettent sous les yeux que la vérité. Je crois au désir d'Oenomaüs pendant son ivresse, je ne regarde pas comme une chose incroyable que deux frères aient pu se combattre l'un l'autre. Et je ne trouvais pas en moi la force de dire que Dieu était l'auteur et le créateur de tous ces maux."*

to the information and the texts in order to complete our depiction of Gnostic thought.

The Followers of the Mother are thus named because nearly all of them accept a female principle as the origin of the world. But even within this rubric, we can include the Barbelo-Gnostics (Barbelo is the name of the female principle), the Orphites of whom Hippolytus speaks, and the "Gnostics" of Irenaeus. They lay stress primarily on the rivalry between the first principle, the Mother, and the male principle, or Iadalboath. The latter created man, and the Mother corrected that which was disastrous in this creation by placing in man a divine seed. Through this the classical history of Redemption was introduced according to Valentinian themes.

The *Philosophumena* cites and comments upon a great number of Gnostics whom it would be vain to want to recall one by one in order to rediscover ideas we have already encountered. It will be easiest to cite those texts which, by their peculiar or curious intentions, will illustrate, as it were, Valentinus's, Basilides', or Marcion's doctrines, as a pastiche often conveys the spirit of a work. At the same time they give us a very precise idea of a way of thinking that was quite common during this strange period, often condemned, yet at times suggestive.

The Naasseni[38] emphasize pessimism regarding the world and are overly meticulous in theology. "This is . . . 'the god that inhabiteth the flood,' according to the Psalter, 'and who speaketh and crieth from many waters.' The 'many waters' . . . are the diversified generation of mortal men, from which (generation) he cries and vociferates to the unportrayed man, saying, 'Preserve my only-begotten from the lions.' In reply to him, it has . . . been declared, 'Israel, thou art my child: fear not, even though thou passest through rivers, they shall not drown thee; even though thou passest through fire, it shall not scorch thee.' "[39]

---

38. This, at least, is the name De Faye gives them.

39. *Philosophumena*, V, 8 [*sic*]: "C'est le Dieu dont parle un Psaume, qui habite le déluge et qui du sein de la multitude des eaux élève la voix et crie. Les eaux, c'est le lieu où sont les générations multiples et variées des hommes mortels. De là il crie vers l'homme qu'aucune forme ne définit, il dit: 'Délivre ton fils unique des lions.' C'est à lui que s'adresse cette parole: 'Tu es mon fils Israël, ne crains pas lorsque tu traverses les fleuves, ils ne te submergeront pas; si tu traverses le feu, il ne te consumera pas."

[Hippolytus, *The Refutation of All Heresies*, 5.3, trans. MacMahon, in *The Ante-Nicene Fathers*, 5:53.—Trans.]

The Peratæ stress Redemption, which consists in an attraction that the Son exercises over all that bears a resemblance to the Father. This is the theory of Paternal Marks: "For as he brought down from above the paternal marks, so again he carries up from thence those marks roused from a dormant condition."[40]

For the Sethians, the superior world is the one of light, while our world is that of darkness. They illustrate our search for the divinity in the following manner: "It is possible to behold an image of the nature of these in the human countenance; for instance, in the pupil of the eye, dark from the subjacent humours, (but) illuminated with spirit. As, then, the darkness seeks after the splendour, that it may keep in bondage the spark, and may have perceptive power, so the light and spirit seek after the power that belongs to themselves, and strive to uprear, and towards each other to carry up their intermingled powers into the dark and formidable water lying underneath."[41] Justinus, the Gnostic of whom Hippolytus speaks, is rather a leader of a religious brotherhood. The sexually symbolic plays a great part in his speculations. It is thus that the world has three parts: the Good God, Elohim the Father Creator, and Edem his wife who represents the world. Tragedy is born when Elohim, drawn to the Good God, abandons Edem. Edem, in order to avenge herself, creates wicked man. Hence the need for Redemption. "Elohim . . . exclaimed, 'Open me the gates, that entering in I may acknowledge the Lord; for I consider Myself to be Lord.' A voice was returned to Him from the light, saying, 'This is the gate of the Lord: through this the righteous enter in.' And immediately the gate was opened, and the Father, without the angels, entered, (advancing) towards the Good One, and beheld 'what eye hath not seen, nor ear hath heard, and what hath not entered into the heart of man to (conceive).' Then the Good One says to him, 'Sit thou on my right hand.' "[42]

40. Ibid., V, 16 [sic]: "comme il a emporté d'en haut les empreintes du Père, de même réciproquement il emporte d'ici là-haut ces empreintes du Père lorsqu'elles ont été réveillées."
[Hippolytus, *The Refutation of All Heresies*, 5.12, ibid., 64.—Trans.]
41. *Philosophumena*, V, 15 [sic]: "L'image de ces choses, c'est la pupille de l'oeil. D'une part, elle est sombre, ce sont les liquides sous-jacents qui l'enténèbrent, d'autre part un pneuma l'illumine: comme les ténèbres de la pupille s'attachent à cette clarté et voudraient la garder et se l'asservir afin de voir, de même la lumière et l'esprit recherchent avec ardeur leur vertu égarée dans les ténèbres."
[Hippolytus, *The Refutation of All Heresies*, 5.14, ibid., 65.—Trans.]
42. Cited by De Faye, [*Gnostiques et Gnosticisme,*] p. 191 [sic]: "Elohim s'écrie: 'Ouvrez-moi les portes afin que j'entre et que je voie le Seigneur. Car je croyais jusqu'ici être le

Finally, we can add to these rather obscure ideas those of a docetic Gnostic who describes Redemption in this way: "After some such manner, that only begotten Son, when He gazes upon the forms of the supernatural Æons, which were transferred from above into darkish bodies, coming down, wished to descend and deliver them. When (the Son), however, became aware that the Æons, those (that subsist) collectively, are unable to hold the Pleroma of all the Æons, but that in a state of consternation they fear lest they may undergo corruption as being themselves perishable, and that they are overwhelmed by the magnitude and splendour of power;—(when the Son, I say, perceived this) he contracted Himself—as it were a very great flash in a very small body, nay, rather as a ray of vision condensed beneath the eyelids, and (in this condition) He advances forth as far as heaven and the effulgent stars. And in this quarter of creation He again collects Himself beneath the lids of vision according as He wishes it . . . He entered into this world just as we have described Him, unnoticed, unknown, obscure, and disbelieved."[43]

If we add to this list a certain Monoïmus the Arab, Neopythagorean and juggler of numbers, we will have a rather good idea of the variety of Gnostic sects and ideas.

We note here only the doctrines of the *Codex Brucianus* and the *Pistis Sophia*, which both reproduce Jesus' discussions, in which classical themes are developed considerably and in which it is explained that to possess gnosis is to know "the reason for light and darkness, chaos, treasure of lights, sin, baptism, anger, blasphemy, injuries, adulteries,

---

Seigneur.' Au sein de la lumière se fait entendre une voix qui disait: 'Voici la porte du Seigneur, les Justes la franchiront.' Aussitôt la porte s'ouvre et le Père, sans les anges, y entre et va vers le Bon. Et il contemple les choses que l'oeil n'a point vues et que l'oreille n'a pas entendues et qui ne sont point montrées au coeur de l'homme. Alors le Bon lui dit: 'Assieds-toi à ma droite'."
[Hippolytus, *The Refutation of All Heresies*, 5.21, ibid., 71.—Trans.]
43. Cited by De Faye, [*Gnostiques et Gnosticisme,*] p. 217 [*sic*]: "Voici comment le Fils Monogène voyant d'en haut les idées transmuées en des corps ténébreux voulut les sauver. Sachant que même les éons ne porraient soutenir la vue du plérôme tout entier, mais que frappés de stupeur, ils en deviendraient mortels et périraient, il se contracta lui-même et réduisit son éclat au plus petit volume; je devrais dire qu'il se fit petit comme la lumière sous les paupières: puis il s'avança jusqu'au ciel visible: il toucha les astres qui s'y trouvent et de nouveau se replia sous les paupières . . . Ainsi est venu dans le monde le Monogène, sans éclat, inconnu, sans gloire: on n'a même pas cru en lui."
[Hippolytus, *The Refutation of All Heresies*, 8.3, ibid., 119–20. The page reference in De Faye should be p. 239.—Trans.]

purity, arrogance, life, malicious gossip, obedience, humility, wealth and slavery."[44]

At this price we will have to leave aside the direct disciples of Valentinus, Heracleon, and Ptolemaeus, Apelles the disciple of Marcion, Marcos and his followers, and the licentious Gnostics. We see, then, the wealth of a movement so often despised. It remains for us to disentangle, in this group of affirmations, whether moving or simply curious, the outside contributions.

II. The Elements of the Gnostic Solution

This metaphysic, which is incarnated, retains its eloquence throughout time. But it cannot lay claim to originality. It seems that in Gnosticism, Christianity, and Hellenism encounter one another without being able to assimilate one another and have therefore placed side by side the most heterogeneous themes. Our task here will be to separate as schematically as possible the outside contributions to Gnosticism.

a) A great number of Gnostic themes appear to come from Plato, or at least from the tradition he represents. The emanation of intelligences from the bosom of the Divinity, the madness and suffering of spirits remote from God and committed to matter, the anxiety of the pure soul tied to the irrational soul in the psychics, regeneration through a return to the original sources, all this is purely Greek. Horos, a significant name, making Sophia return within the limits of her nature is typical in this regard.

Greece introduced the notions of order and harmony into morality as into æsthetics. If Prometheus has suffered, it is because he has cast off his human nature. Sophia acted likewise, and it is by returning to the place which she was assigned that she once again finds peace.

b) Furthermore, Gnosticism has taken from Christianity the essence of its dogmas. It is happy to make use of them. Nevertheless, any Gnostic

---

44. Cited by De Faye, [*Gnostiques et Gnosticisme,*] p. 269 [*sic*].
[The text Camus quotes here is neither from the *Codex Brucianus* nor the *Pistis Sophia,* but rather is De Faye's own commentary on the latter. The actual page reference in De Faye is p. 291.—Trans.]

system is accompanied by a few ideas the echos of which we cannot mistake. The concern of all our authors is the problem of evil; we have seen it in Basilides, Marcion, and Valentinus. Hence their attempt also to explain Redemption.

Another influence, less marked but just as true, is the meaning of history, that is to say, the idea that the world marches toward a goal as if it were the conclusion of a tragedy. In this view of history, the world is a point of departure. It was a beginning. Truths are not to be contemplated. Rather, we use them and with them achieve our salvation. Here the Christian influence resides less in a group of doctrines than in a state of mind and an orientation. In no other doctrine has the irreducible in man held such explanatory value.

c) But to these influences were added very diverse elements, which were thereby less shocking and upon which we will expand a little, that which precedes having been illustrated in our account of the Gnostic doctrines.

1) In this notion of a higher science that constitutes gnosis we can also see the influence of the mysteries. We have already defined initiation as the union of knowledge and salvation. We encounter the same problem here. A "spiritual" being would make his own these orphic lines, found on the gold tablets at Croton: "I have escaped from the circle of trouble and sadness and I am now advancing toward the queen of sovereign places, Saint Persephone, and the other divinities of Hades. I glory in belonging to their blessed race. I ask them to send me into the dwelling places of the innocent in order to receive there the saving word: You will be a goddess and no longer mortal."[45]

2) A more suggestive coincidence is the one that links the Gnostics to Philo.[46] Philo occasionally prophesies like an initiate. "Let them who corrupt religion into superstition close their ears or depart. For this is a

---

45. In Toussaint, *Saint Paul et l'Hellénisme*, ch. I: "Je me suis enuie du cercle des peines et des tristesses et maintenant je m'avance vers la reine des lieux souverains, la sainte Perséphone et les autres divinités de l'Hadès. Je me glorifie d'appartenir à leur race bienheureuse. Je leur demande de m'envoyer dans la demeure des innocents pour y recevoir le mot sauveur: Tu seras déesse et non plus mortelle."*

[The title of Toussaint's work is *L'Hellénisme et l'Apôtre Paul*.—Trans.]

46. [For a discussion of Camus' analysis of Philo and his role in the advent of Gnosticism, see my "Albert Camus on Philo and Gnosticism," in *The Studia Philonica Annual: Studies in Hellenistic Judaism*, vol. 7, ed. David T. Runia (Atlanta: Scholars Press, 1995), 103–6.—Trans.]

divine mystery and its lesson is for the initiated who are worthy to receive the holiest secret, even those who in simplicity of heart practise the piety which is true and genuine, free from all tawdry ornament."[47]

Consider this still more significant passage: "These thoughts, ye initiated, whose ears are purified, receive into your souls as holy mysteries indeed and babble not of them to any of the profane. Rather as stewards guard the treasure in your own keeping, not where gold and silver, substances corruptible, are stored, but where lies that most beautiful of all possessions, the knowledge of the Cause and of virtue, and, besides these two, of the fruit which is engendered by them both."[48]

Consequently, we should not be surprised to find with the Gnostics a rather large number of themes dear to Philo: the supreme Being, source of light that shines forth through the universe,[49] the battle between light and darkness for control of the world, the creation of the world by intermediaries, the visible world as an image of the invisible world, the theme (essential for Philo) of the image of God as the unadulterated essence of the human soul, and deliverance finally, allotted as the goal of human existence.[50]

3) Finally, it is possible to recognize within Gnostic doctrines the influence of a certain number of Oriental speculations, especially of Avesta. Zoroastrianism, moreover, as a result of the exile of the Jews, of the protection that Cyrus accorded them and the benevolence that he had shown Avesta, played a considerable role in the evolution of ideas in the first centuries of our era.

The Ameshas Spentas and the Yazatas, who maintain the fight against wicked demons, themselves also constitute a pleroma, intermediate

47. From Cherubin, pp. 115–16; Matter, *Histoire du Gnosticisme,* I, ch. V: "Que les hommes bornés se retirent, les oreilles bouchées. Nous transmettons des mystères divins à ceux qui ont reçu l'initiation sacrée, à ceux qui pratiquent une piété véritable, qui ne sont pas enchaînés par le vain apparat des mots ou le prestige des païens."
[Philo, *On the Cherubim,* 42, vol. 2, ed. T. E. Page, trans. F. H. Colson and G. H. Whitaker, Loeb Classical Library (Cambridge: Harvard University Press, 1929), 35.—Trans.]

48. Ibid., M. Matter: "O vous initiés, vous dont les oreilles sont purifiées, recevez cela dans votre âme comme des mystères qui n'en doivent jamais sortir. Ne le révélez à aucun profane; cachez-le et gardez-le dans vous-même, comme un trésor qui n'est point corruptible, à l'instar de l'or et de l'argent, mais qui est plus précieux que toute autre chose, puisque c'est la science de la grande cause de la vertu et de ce qui naît de l'un et de l'autre."
[Philo, *On the Cherubim,* 48, vol. 2, ibid., 37.—Trans.]

49. Cf. Bréhier, *Les idées philosophiques et religieuses de Philon d'Alexandrie,* part II: "Dieu, les Intermédiaires et le Monde."

50. Ibid., part III: "Le culte spirituel et le progrès moral."

between God and the earth. And Ahura Mazda has all the characteristics of the infinite Gnostic God.

These indications suffice to bring to light the complexity of Gnosticism. We see the medley of colors from which this Christian heresy shone forth. Again it is necessary to attempt to summarize our investigations in a few general characteristics.

Conclusion

Gnosticism in the Evolution of Christianity

"Instead of eternal acts of the divine will, dramatic climaxes or passionate initiatives; failures replacing causes; in place of the unity of two natures in the person of Christ incarnated, the dispersion of divine particles in matter; instead of the distinction between eternity and time, a time saturated with eternal influences and an eternity shot through with, and emphasized by, tragedy."[51]

It would be best to sum up the spirit of Gnosticism thus: extending over more than two centuries, it gathers up all the ideas that lingered about the period in order to form an outrageous Christianity, woven from Oriental religions and Greek mythology. But that this heresy was Christian we cannot doubt by a certain raucous resonance that runs through it. It is evil that obsessed the Gnostics. They are all pessimists regarding the world. It is with great ardor that they address a God whom they nevertheless make inaccessible. But Christianity draws from this emotion, incalculable in the face of the divinity, the idea of His omnipotence and of man's nothingness. Gnosticism sees in knowledge a means of salvation. In that it is Greek, because it wants that which illuminates to restore at the same time. What it develops is a Greek theory of grace.

Historically, Gnosticism reveals to Christianity the path not to follow. It is because of its excesses that Tertullian and Tatian check Christianity in its march toward the Mediterranean. It is, to a certain extent, because of Gnosticism that Christian thought will take from the Greeks only their formulas and their structures of thought—not their sentimental

---

51. J. Guitton, *Le Temps et l'Éternité chez Plotin et Saint Augustin,* chap. II, I, p. 27.

postulates, which are neither reducible to Evangelical thought nor capable of being juxtaposed to it—but without the slightest coherence. Perhaps it is already clear that Christianity, introduced into the Greco-Roman world at the end of the first century, did not make any decisive development until the milieu of the third century. We understand as well the importance we have accorded to the Gnostic doctrines regarding the evolution we want to recount. Gnosticism shows us one of the Greco-Christian combinations that were possible. It marks an important stage, an experience we could not pass over in silence.

The excesses themselves make us better aware of the risk of being lost in details and nuances. Nevertheless, Christianity fought this undergrowth mercilessly. But it is harder to rid oneself of one's false children than of one's enemies. Moreover, through a remarkable sense of History, the Fathers seemed to understand which work was going to be jeopardized by similar excesses, however moving they often were: namely, the march of Christianity toward the role for which it had been destined. But let us leave Christian thought waiting at this turning point in its history. Parallel to these developments in Christian thought, Alexandrian metaphysics was crystalizing in this period in Neoplatonism, and the material that dogmatic Christianity will use is in the process of being developed. Thus is developing, in different directions, that second revelation, which was Augustinian doctrine.

Chapter Three

Mystic Reason

I. Plotinus's Solution

Regarding our subject, a study of Plotinus is interesting in a double sense. For the first time, the problem upon which the fate of Christianity rests is clearly set out. Moreover, the Plotinian synthesis supplies Christian thought, not with a doctrine (as certain authors argue), but with a method and a way of seeing things. The Plotinian system actually stands out against a background of religious and mystical aspirations common to the whole period. It often adopts even the language of the mysteries.[1] The desire for God is what animates Plotinus.[2] But he is also a Greek, and very determined to remain so to the extent that he is content to be nothing more than Plato's commentator.[3] In vain, however. His World Soul is Stoic. His Intelligible world comes from Aristotle. And his synthesis retains a completely personal tone. But it

---

1. Compare *Ennead* I, "seuls l'obtiennent . . . ceux qui se dépouillent de leurs vêtements," and the description of the journey of the soul in the mysteries of Mithra, M. Cumont, *Les Mystères de Mithra,* pp. 114 and *sq.*

[The text Camus cites appears to be from *Ennead* 1.6.7: "just as for those who go up to the celebration of sacred rites there are purifications, and strippings off of the clothes they wore before, and going up naked." Plotinus, *Ennead* 1.6.7, ed. T. E. Page, trans. A. H. Armstrong, Loeb Classical Library (Cambridge: Harvard University Press, 1964), 253. Subsequent citations are to the Loeb edition.—Trans.]

2. Cf. Arnou, *Le Désir de Dieu dans la philosophie de Plotin.*

3. *Enneads* III, 7, 13; V, 1, 9.

remains true that he has a liking for rational explanations of things. And it is in this that his personal tragedy also reflects the drama of Christian metaphysics. He is concerned about the destiny of the soul;[4] but following his master, he also wants destiny to be included in the intellectual forms.[5] The conceptual material has not changed with Plotinus; it is just that emotion is busy with new investigations. The whole fragrance of the Plotinian landscape is this: a certain tragedy in this attempt to cast emotion in the logical forms of Greek idealism. From this, and from the point of view of style, comes this slowness, this advance by degrees, this apparent mastery that gives birth instead to a freely accepted shackle. From this also is derived the profound originality of Plotinus's solution and the grandeur of his enterprise. For, to see clearly, Plotinus himself proposed to create, without the assistance of Faith and with the resources of Greek philosophy alone, what ten centuries of Christianity have succeeded in creating with great difficulty.

This explains a sort of shimmering in the thought of our author. To tell the truth, each Plotinian doctrine reveals a double aspect whose coincidence determines precisely a solution to the problem we have indicated above. This solution is the joining of the destiny of the soul and the rational knowledge of things. Here the solution is like it is in psychoanalysis: the diagnosis coincides with the treatment. To reveal is to know and to cure oneself, it is to restore one's homeland. "The demonstrations [of the Good] themselves were a kind of leading up on our way."[6]

It is through that device that we will take up the study of Plotinus. We will attempt to retrieve that double aspect at each point in his doctrine. But we notice already how much his solution depends on his conception of Reason. To know is to worship in accordance with Reason. Science is a form of contemplation and inner meditation, not a construction. Of

---

4. Cf. *Ennead* I, 1, 12: "L'âme ne peut pécher. Pourquoi alors les châtiments?"
[Plotinus *Ennead* 1.1.12: "But if the soul is sinless, how is it judged?" *Ennead* 1, trans. Armstrong, 117.—Trans.]

5. *Ennead* I, 2, 2: "Car un être devient meilleur parce qu'il se limite et parce que, soumis à la mesure, il sort du domaine des êtres privés de mesure et de limite."
[Plotinus *Ennead* 1.2.2: "The civic virtues, which we mentioned above, do genuinely set us in order and make us better by giving limit and measure to our desires, and putting measure into all our experience." Ibid., 133.—Trans.]

6. *Ennead* I, 3, 1: "Les démonstrations qu'on en donne [du Bien] sont aussi des moyens de s'élever jusqu'à lui."
[Plotinus *Ennead* 1.3.1, ibid., 153.—Trans.]

course, Plotinus's rationalism is based on the intelligibility of the world—but with what endless flexibility. The principles or hypostases that underlie this intelligibility are valid only in a perpetual motion that leads them from cosmological explanation to the particular state of grace that each of them represents. In one sense they mark the order of a procession, in another sense they reveal the path of conversion. To a certain extent, Plotinian Reason is already the "heart" of Pascal. But this does not mean that we can equate it with Christian thought, because this conception of Reason, being based on contemplation, is inscribed in an æsthetic: as well as a form of religious thought, Plotinus's philosophy is an artist's point of view. If things are explained, it is because the things are beautiful. But Plotinus carries over into the intelligible world this extreme emotion that seizes the artist confronted with the beauty of the world. He admires the universe to the detriment of nature. "All that is here below comes from there [the intelligible world], and exists in greater beauty there."[7] It is not the appearance that Plotinus seeks but rather the inside of things, which is his lost paradise. Each thing here below is made a living reminder of this solitary homeland of the wise. This is why Plotinus describes intelligence in a sensual way.[8] His Reason is alive, fleshed out, stirring like a mixture of water and light: "as if there was one quality which held and kept intact all the qualities in itself, of sweetness along with fragrance, and was at once the quality of wine and the characters of all tastes, the sights of colours and all the awareness of touch, and all that hearings hear, all tunes and every rhythm."[9] It is therefore with his sensitivity that Plotinus seizes the intelligible.

But this, which might make one believe in a point of contact between Christianity and Neoplatonism, appears to us, on the contrary, as one of insurmountable oppositions. To stake all on contemplation is only

---

7. *Ennead* V, 8, 7: "Tout ce qui ici-bas vient de là-haut, est plus beau dans le monde supérieur."
[Plotinus *Ennead* 5.8.7, trans. Armstrong, 259.—Trans.]
8. Cf. also the abuse of the "Metaphysic of Light" in Plotinus. The light is that which is the limit of the corporeal and the incorporeal.
9. *Ennead* VI, 7, 12: "comme une qualité unique, qui a et conserve en elle toutes les autres, une douceur qui serait en même temps une odeur, en qui la saveur du vin s'unirait à toutes les autres saveurs et toutes les autres couleurs; elle a toutes les qualités qui sont perçues par le tact et aussi toutes celles qui sont perçues par l'oreille puisqu'elle est toute harmonie et tout rythme."
[Plotinus *Ennead* 6.7.12, trans. Armstrong, 127.—Trans.]

valid for a world that is once and for all eternal and harmonious. Hence, for Plotinus, this is not the contemplation of History. But for a Christian, art does not suffice. The world unfolds according to a divine production; and to be restored is to be incorporated into the movement of this tragedy. The climax of the Incarnation has no meaning for Plotinus. This is an opposition that goes still further. For the Christian who separates Reason and Beauty, the Truth of Beauty, Reason is reduced to its role of logical legislator. And thus conflicts between Faith and Reason become possible. For a Greek, these conflicts are less acute, because Beauty, which is both order and sensitivity, economy and the object of passion, remains a ground of agreement. "If someone who sees beauty excellently represented in a face is carried to that higher world, will anyone be so sluggish in mind and so immovable that, when he sees all the beauties in the world of sense, all its good proportion and the mighty excellence of its order, and the splendour of form which is manifested in the stars, for all their remoteness, he will not thereupon think, seized with reverence, 'What wonders, and from what source?' If he did not, he would neither have understood this world here nor seen the higher world."[10] We have already noted this passage. It is directed against the Gnostic Christians.

A. *The Rational Explanation according to Procession*

a) If the world is beautiful, it is because something lives in it. But it is also because something orders it. This spirit that animates the world is the World Soul. The superior principle that limits this life within determined structures is called Intelligence. But the unity of an order is always superior to that order. Thus there exists a third principle superior to Intelligence, which is the One. Let us argue this in an inverse direction. There is no being that is not one.[11] Now there is no unity without form

---

10. *Ennead* II, 9, 16: "Il en est qui voyant l'image de la beauté sur un visage sont transportés dans l'intelligible; d'autres ont une pensée trop paresseuse et rien ne les émeut; ils ont beau regarder toutes les beautés du monde sensible, ses proportions, sa régularité, et le spectacle qu'offrent les Astres malgré leur éloignement, ils ne songeront pas, saisis d'un respect religieux, à dire: 'Que c'est beau, et de quelle beauté doit venir leur beauté.' C'est qu'ils n'ont compris ni les choses sensibles ni les êtres intelligibles."
[Plotinus *Enneads* 2.9.16, trans. Armstrong, 291.—Trans.]
11. *Ennead* VI, 9, 1.

and without logos, logos rightly being the principle of unity. That is to say, once more, that there is no being without soul, since logos is the necessary action of the soul. In the first meaning we have discovered three levels in the explanation of the world; in the second, three stages of deepening the Self. These two processes coincide.[12] Metaphysical reality is spiritual life considered in itself. The first is the object of knowledge; the second, of inner asceticism. And where objects coincide, so too do methods. To know is to return somewhat to the "more inward than my most inward part."[13] Knowledge is not an experience, but an effort and a desire, in a word, a creative evolution. Here again we see the divine character of metaphysical principles. The One, Intelligence, and the World Soul express the same divinity, the first in its fullness, the other two as a reflection. The procession of the three hypostases shows how this unity and this multiplicity are reconciled. This hypostatic progression, which underlies the rational explanation of the world, naturally finds its equal in conversion, which is the very movement of the soul in search of its origins.[14]

Let us indicate only the movement of this procession, setting aside for the moment a detailed examination of each of its moments.

"All things which exist, as long as they remain in being, necessarily produce from their own substances, in dependence on their present powers . . . [thus] fire produces the heat which comes from it; snow does not only keep its cold inside itself."[15]

God himself, insofar as he is perfect substance and timeless, superabounds. He creates Intelligence, and from Intelligence will arise the World Soul.

It is in this way that Intelligence and Soul both are and are not the One. They are the One in their origin and not in their outcome, in which

12. Cf. above all this passage: for the religious role of the hypostases, *Ennead* V, 1, "On the Three Primary Hypostases." Cf. on their explicative value, *Ennead* V, 3, "On the Knowing Hypostases."

13. ["I'intimior intinio meo" (*sic*). Camus offers no reference for this text. It is from Saint Augustine, *Confessions,* trans. Henry Chadwick (Oxford: Oxford University Press, 1991), 3.6.11. The Latin text should read: "intimor intimo meo."—Trans.]

14. *Ennead* VI, 6 [*sic*]: "Tout être engendré désire et aime l'être qui l'a engendré." [Plotinus *Enneads* 5.1.6: "Everything longs for its parent and loves it." *Ennead* 5, trans. Armstrong, 33.—Trans.]

15. *Ennead* V, 1, 6: "Tous les êtres d'ailleurs, tant qu'ils subsistent, produisent nécessairement autour d'eux, de leur propre essence, une réalité qui tend vers l'extérieur et dépend de leur pouvoir actuel . . . ainsi le feu fait naître de la chaleur et la neige ne garde pas en elle-même tout son froid."
[Plotinus *Enneads* 5.1.6, ibid., 31.—Trans.]

they are divided, the one into duality, the other into multiplicity. "The One is all things and not a single one of them: it is the principle of all things, not all things, [but all things have that other kind of transcendent existence; for in a way they do occur in the One;] or rather they are not there yet, but they will be."[16]

We see here how the notion of procession is opposed to that of creation: the latter separating the heavens and the creator, the former unifying them in the same gentle movement of superabundance. But this divine emanation does not take form until Intelligence, descended from God, turns back toward him and receives his reflection, and until the Soul, in its turn, contemplates the intelligible sun and is illuminated by it. It is therefore through contemplation of the superior hypostasis that each principle is fully realized.[17] Here God allows only his admirers to live. But this, scarcely noted, needs to be examined in detail.

b) *The First Hypostasis.* Let us confront in succession the ambiguity already indicated in the notion of the One. It is simultaneously a rational principle of explanation and a desire of the soul. Plato says that the Good is the greatest of the sciences: by science he means, not the vision of the Good, but the reasoned knowledge that we had of it before this vision.

What educates us about the Good are analogies, negations, and knowledge of beings descended from it and their graduated ascent. But what leads us to it are our purifications, our virtues, and our inner order.

Thus one becomes a contemplator of oneself and other things, and at the same time, the object of one's contemplation; and having become essence, intelligence, and animal together, one no longer sees the good from outside.[18]

Notice that these two aspects are not coexistent but identical. What constitutes the first hypostasis is the principle of unity; it is the fact that we contemplate it.[19] At the very moment when we look at a star, it

---

16. *Ennead* V, 2, 1: "L'un est toutes les choses et il n'est aucune d'entre elles; principe de toutes choses car toutes font en quelque sorte retour à lui; ou, plutôt à son niveau, elles ne sont pas encore mais elles seront."

[Plotinus *Ennead* 5.2.1, ibid., 59. The portion of the text in square brackets is not included in Camus' quotation. I have added it in order to clarify the meaning of the passage.—Trans.]

17. *Ennead* V, 1, 6; V, 2; V, 3, 4.

18. *Ennead* VI, 7, 35.

19. *Ennead* III, 8, 10.

defines us and limits us to a certain extent. And to say that the One is the principle of all things is to say that contemplation is the sole reality.

If we now attempt to define this One, we come up against a good many difficulties.

1) In the first place, the One is nothing, not being distinct, being pure unity. But it is everything, as the principle of all things. Indeed, it is the Beautiful and the Good together.[20] But these are not definitions. They are ways of speaking that do not bind the Good, because clearly, it is only a nothing, or, at most, a point of convergence.[21] But at bottom the difficulty is not here. The real question is this: Why has the One, which contains all reality contracted within itself, created, and above all how is this unity made a multiplicity?

2) "The One, perfect because it seeks nothing, has nothing, and needs nothing, overflows, as it were, and its superabundance makes something other than itself. This, when it has come into being, turns back upon the One and is filled, and becomes Intellect by looking toward it. Its halt and turning toward the One constitutes being, its gaze upon the One, Intellect. Since it halts and turns toward the One that it may see, it becomes at once Intellect and being."[22] The One, therefore, produces Intellect and being as fire gives off heat or a flower its fragrance. And it is as an object of contemplation that the One gives Intelligence the forms in which it is clothed.[23] But how can we accept that this One is

---

20. *Ennead* I, 6, 6: "Il faut donc rechercher par des moyens analogues le Bien et le Beau, le Laid et le Mal. Il faut poser d'abord que la Beauté est aussi le Bien."
[Plotinus *Ennead* 1.6.6: "So we must follow the same line of inquiry to discover beauty and goodness, and ugliness and evil. And first we must posit beauty which is also the good." *Ennead* 1, trans. Armstrong, 251.—Trans.]

21. *Enneads* VI, 8, 9; V, 1, 6.

22. *Ennead* VI, 2 [*sic*]: "L'un étant parfait surabonde et cette surabondance produit une chose différente de lui; la chose engendrée se retourne vers lui; elle est fécondée; et, en tournant son regard sur elle-même, elle devient intelligence; son arrêt, par rapport à lui, la produit comme intelligence. Et puisqu'elle s'est arrêtée pour se regarder elle-même, elle devient à la fois intelligence et être."
[Plotinus *Ennead* 5.2.1, trans. Armstrong, 59.—Trans.]

23. Cf. also *Ennead* VI, 7 [*sic*]: "Au moment oè la vie dirige sur lui ses regards, elle est illimitée; une fois qu'elle l'a vu, elle se limite . . . Ce regards vers l'Un apporte immédiatement en elle la limite, la détermination et la forme . . . ; cette vie qui a reçu une limite c'est l'Intelligence."
[Plotinus *Ennead* 6.7.17: "So when its life was looking towards that it was unlimited, but after it had looked there it was limited . . . For immediately by looking to something which is one the life is limited by it, and has in itself limit and bound and form . . . for life defined and limited is intellect." *Ennead* 6, trans. Armstrong, 142–43.—Trans.]

scattered throughout a multiplicity of intelligibles? Herein lies the true difficulty and the center of the Plotinian system. For this problem is linked to the further problem, no less important, of divine Transcendence or Immanence, and to those that posit relationships between Intelligence and the intelligible, or between the World Soul and individual souls. And it is precisely here that there intervenes a certain way of seeing, particular to Plotinus, one that we will have to define at the end of our study.

At times, Plotinus is content to describe the mechanism of the operation: "That Good is the principle, and it is from that that they are in this Intellect, and it is this which has made them from that Good. For it was not lawful in looking to him to think nothing, nor again to think what was in him; for then Intellect itself would not have generated them. Intellect therefore had the power from him to generate and to be filled full of its own offspring, since the Good gave what he did not himself have. *But from the Good himself who is one there were many for this Intellect; for it was unable to hold the power which it received and broke it up and made the one power many, that it might be able so to bear it part by part.*"[24] But if, from the description, Plotinus passes over to the explanation, he has recourse to images. How can the One both be and not be dispersed in multiplicity? As a tree is spread out among its branches without being found in them entirely,[25] as light is dispersed in the rays it emits without, however, being gathered together in them,[26] as fire gives off heat and communicates it by affinity,[27] and finally, as a source is able to give birth to rivers that will run to a sea of different yet similar waters,[28] this is how the One both is and is not dispersed in multiplicity. Stated differently, the principle of contradiction could be used

---

24. *Ennead* VI, 7, 15: "Le Bien est principe. C'est de lui que 'Intelligence tient les êtres qu'elle produit. Quand elle les regarde il n'est pas plus permis à l'Intelligence de ne rien penser que de penser ce qui est en lui; sinon elle n'engendrerait pas. De l'Un, elle tient la puissance d'engendrer et de se rassasier des êtres qu'elle engendre; il lui donne ce qu'il ne possède pas lui-même. De l'Un naît pour l'Intelligence une multiplicité: incapable de contenir la puissance qu'elle reçoit de lui, elle la fragmente et la multiplie, afin de pouvoir la supporter ainsi, partie par partie."

[Plotinus *Ennead* 6.7.15, ibid., 135–37. I have matched Camus' emphasis in the English translation.—Trans.]

25. *Ennead* V, 5, 2, end.
26. *Ennead* V, 1, 6.
27. *Ennead* V, 4, 1.
28. *Ennead* III, 8, 10.

if it were a question of creation, but under the category of procession, it is necessary to appeal to another principle, one very similar to that principle of participation that Levy Bruhl attributes only to primitive mentalities. But it is in the interior of the intelligible world that one must attempt to understand this particular solution.

c) *The Second Hypostasis.* On the rational plane, which we are here attempting to consider almost exclusively, is Intelligence, which is endowed with the greatest explanatory power. Moreover, the theory is not itself completely fixed. We can begin by noting a double aspect that is already classic for us. Intelligence is a metaphysical principle but remains a stage in the repatriation of the soul. In the first aspect, it is identified with the world of platonic Ideas. But within even this last notion, we can detect three interpretations juxtaposed to the second hypostasis. Intelligence is, in the first place, a kind of intuitive art that is reflected in the world's crystal, as the art of the sculptor is divined in very rough-hewn clay. Second, it is the perfect model upon which the Forms are moulded. And last, it is a God, or rather a demiurge, who has given form to matter. But we must be careful not to exaggerate this diversity of interpretation. And here let us take the notion of Intelligence in its broadest meaning of the world of ideas. At this point a problem arises that is closely related to the one we saw in the theory of the One, namely, the problem of how the Intelligence pours itself into the intelligibles. Are the intelligibles different from Intelligence, or are they inwardly of a form that is common to both?

Plotinus's solution is the notion of transparency. The intelligibles are within Intelligence, but their relations are not those that ordinary logic would accept. Like those diamonds that the same water covers, of which each flash is nourished by fires that also reflect on other surfaces, such that this infinitely repeated light is defined only by these fires but at the same time without being able to embody them, in this way Intelligence scatters its brilliance in the intelligibles that are in it, as it is in them, without one being able to say what it is of Intelligence that belongs to them and what of them belongs to it. "All things there are transparent, and there is nothing dark or opaque; everything and all things are clear to the inmost part to everything; for light itself is transparent to light. Each there has everything in itself and sees all things in every other, so that all are everywhere and each and every one is all and the glory is unbounded . . . the sun there is all the stars, and each star is the sun and all others. A different kind of being stands out in each, but in each all are manifest . . . Here, however, one part would not come from another, and each would be only a part; but there each comes only from the whole and is part and whole at once."[29] What stands out in these remarks is that Intelligence bears within it all the wealth of the intelligible world. To know, for Intelligence, is entirely in knowing itself—and through that, knowing the One. In this idea is found the Unity of the second hypostasis, however one may envisage it. But at precisely this point thought changes levels in order to enter into conversion and inner asceticism, which we have not yet taken into consideration. Let us note only that in the ideal, Intelligence indicates a state in which the object is identified

29. *Ennead* II, 8, 4 [*sic*]: "Tout est transparent, rien d'obscur ni de résistant; tout être y est visible à tout être jusque dans son infinité; il est une lumière pour une lumière. Tout être a en lui toutes choses et voit toutes choses en autrui. Tout est partout. Tout est tout. Chaque être est tout. Là-bas, le soleil est tous les astres et chacun d'eux est le soleil . . . Un caractères s'y manifestent . . . Ici-bas une partie vient d'une autre partie, et chaque chose est fragmentaire: là-bas chaque être vient à chaque instant du tout et il est à la fois particulier et universel." Also, we cite in a note, due to its length, a suggestive text, by its image and meaning, on this aspect of Plotinian thought. Ibid., VI, 8, 9 [*sic*]: "Supposez que dans votre monde visible chaque partie reste ce qu'elle est sans confusion, mais que toutes se rassemblent en une, de telle sorte qui si l'une d'entre elles apparaît, par exemple la sphère des fixes, il s'ensuit immédiatement l'apparition du soleil et des autres astres; l'on voit en elle, comme sur une sphère transparente, la terre, la mer et tous les animaux; effectivement alors, on y voit toutes choses. Soit donc, dans l'âme, la représentation d'une telle sphère. Gardez-en l'image et représentez-vous une autre sphère pareille en faisant abstraction de sa masse; faites abstraction aussi des différences de position et de l'image de la matière; ne vous contentez pas de vous représenter une seconde sphère plus petite que la première . . . Dieu vient alors, nous apportant son propre monde uni à tous les dieux qui sont en lui. Tous sont chacun et chacun est tous; tous ensemble ils sont différents par leurs puissances; mais ils sont tous un être unique avec une puissance multiple."

[Plotinus, *Ennead* 5.8.4, trans. Armstrong, 249–51. The second passage is actually taken from *Ennead* 5.8.9: "Let us then apprehend in our thought this visible universe, with each of its parts remaining what it is without confusion, gathering all of them together into one as far as we can, so that when any one part appears first, for instance the outside heavenly sphere, the imagination of the sun and, with it, the other heavenly bodies follow immediately, and the earth and sea and all the living creatures are seen, as they could in fact all be seen inside a transparent sphere. Let there be, then, in the soul a shining imagination of a sphere, having everything within it, either moving or standing still, or some things moving and others standing still. Keep this, and apprehend in your mind another, taking away the mass: take away also the places, and the mental picture of matter in yourself, and do not try to apprehend another sphere smaller in mass than the original one, [but calling on the god who made that of which you have the mental picture, pray him to come]. And may he come, bringing his own universe with him, with all the gods within him, he who is one and all, and each god is all the gods coming together into one; they are different in their powers, but by that one manifold power they are all one" (ibid., 265–67). It was necessary to add the section of this passage which Camus himself omits in order to make its meaning clear.—Trans.]

with the subject, in which pure thought is only thought of itself. It is by a progressive concentration, by diving into itself, that Intelligence takes hold of its inner wealth. Do we want to go further? Again Plotinus appeals to an image: "[The unbounded is in Intellect in this way, that it is one as one-many, not like one lump but like a rational forming principle multiple in itself,] in the one figure of Intellect holding as within an outline outlines inside itself and again figurations inside powers and thoughts; and its division does not go in a straight line, but moves always to the interior, as the natures of living beings are included in and belong to the smaller living things and the weaker powers, where it will come to a stop at the indivisible form."[30] It is through the reshaping of the enclosure that Intelligence takes hold of its most profound truth. This Being that lies at the bottom of all things, that gives to the world its existence and its true meaning, draws all of its unity from its origin. And scattered in its intelligibles though being known as Intelligence, it is the ideal intermediary between the indefinable Good that we hope for and the Soul that breathes behind sensible appearances.

d) *The Third Hypostasis.*[31] "It occupies a middle rank among realities, belonging to that divine part but being on the lowest edge of the intelligible, and, having a common boundary with the perceptible nature, gives something to it of what it has in itself and receives something from it in return, if it does not use only its safe part in governing the universe, but with greater eagerness plunges into the interior and does not stay whole with whole."[32] In Plotinian terms, to explain a costly notion

---

30. *Ennead* VI, 7, 14: "Dans la figure unique de l'Intelligence qui est comme une enceinte se trouvent des enceintes intérieures qui limitent d'autres figures; il s'y trouve des puissances, des pensées et une subdivision qui ne va pas en ligne droite mais la divise intérieurement, comme un animal universel qui comprend d'autres animaux puis d'autres encore jusqu'aux animaux et aux puissances qui ont le moins d'extension, c'est-à-dire jusqu'à l'espèce indivisible où elle s'arrête."
[Plotinus *Ennead* 6.7.14, trans. Armstrong, 133.—Trans.]

31. Principal texts: a) in general: *Enneads* IV, 3, 4, 5. b) definition: I, 8, 14; III, 4, 3; IV, 6, 31; IV, 8, 7; IV, 8, 3; VI, 7, 35. c) analysis: III, 8, 5; IV, 3, 4, 9; IV, 9. d) relation between World Soul and individual souls: III, 1, 14; IV, 3, 5, and 6; IV, 3, 12; IV, 3, 17; IV, 8, 6; IV, 9, 8; VI, 1, 2; V, 2, 7; VI, 4, 16; VI, 5, 7; VI, 1, 7.

32. *Ennead* IV, 8, 7: "C'est qu'elle occupe dans les êtres un rang intermédiaire; elle a une portion d'elle-même qui est divisée: mais placée à l'extrémité des êtres intelligibles et aux confins de la nature sensible, elle lui donne quelque chose d'elle-même. Elle reçoit en échange quelque chose de cette nature, si elle ne l'organise pas en restant elle-même en sûreté et si par trop d'ardeur elle se plonge en elle sans rester en entier en elle-même."
[Plotinus *Ennead* 4.8.7, trans. Armstrong, 419.—Trans.]

amounts to circumscribing the exact place where it is inserted into the current of the hypostases. This text explains clearly the first aspect of the soul, heir of the intelligible world in its superior part, and dipping its lower extremity into the sensible world. But at the same time the religious content of this conception appears, and we see how the soul, a metaphysical principle, could be equally able to serve as a basis for a theory of the fall or of original sin.

This World Soul defines all that lives, in the style of the Animal of the Stoic world. But at the same time, it is also the intelligible world and more and more divided and fragmented (as the latter marks already the dispersion of the One). It is therefore the intermediary between the sensible world and the intelligible world. In its relations with the intelligible world there are few difficulties. Intelligence produces the Soul as the One has engendered Intelligence itself.[33] But if it is true that the World Soul is dispersed in the sensible world, if it is true that individual souls are parts of the World Soul that are given to play, in their respective spheres, the role that the World Soul itself maintains in the theater of the world,[34] how can these parts and this whole be reconciled? And this continuity of principles and Beings that gives all its meaning to the Plotinian doctrine, how will it be maintained? A new problem arises regarding the soul just as one arose for the first two hypostases.

1) Plotinus has considered this hypostasis as particularly important, seeing that he devotes to it especially three treatises of *Ennead* IV.[35] Again the most sure way for us to proceed is to refer to these treatises. They envisage two problems: the relations of the World Soul to individual souls, and the relation of the human soul to its body. The latter relation, which deals particularly with psychology, will be studied in its turn and will serve as a completely natural transition to our study of conversion.

In the ninth treatise of *Ennead* IV, Plotinus demonstrates the fundamental unity of souls and their liaison with the force that animates the world. To tell the truth, above all he gives them an image. He represents this unity as that of a seminal reason encompassing all bodily organs or defines it as a science encompassing potentially all its theorems.[36] But

33. *Ennead* V, 4, 2.
34. *Ennead* III, 2, 3.
35. *Ennead* IV, 3, 4, 5: "On Difficulties about the Soul."
36. *Ennead* IV, 9, 5.

this being established, there arises the question of the production of individual souls. Plotinus's solution is, as always, less a reason than a sentiment of which he attempts to provide the equivalent in an image— a solution already utilized for the One and Intelligence, and the essence of which, according to Breheir, comes down to "the affirmation of a unity between souls that are not a confusion and the affirmation of a confusion that is not a division."[37] Here again the image of light intervenes.[38]

Or consider this further image: "So it is also in All, to whatever it reaches; it is in one part of a plant and also in another, even if it is cut off; so that it is in the original plant and the part cut off from it: for the body of the all is one, and soul is everywhere in it as in one thing."[39] How, then, does Plotinus explain the differences between individual souls? "It is that they do not have the same relation to the intelligible. They are more or less opaque. And this lesser transparency, which renders them different on the path of the procession, organizes them into a hierarchy on the path of conversion. In this connection the explanation by contemplation forcefully intervenes."[40] "[It was said that all souls are all things, but each is differentiated according to that which is active in it: that is, by] one being united in actuality, one being in a state of knowledge, one in a state of desire, and in that different souls look at different things and are and become what they look at."[41]

2) To sum up, the complete unity of souls is a unity of convergence by which they all participate in the same living reality. Their multiplicity is that of a spiritual life that is obscured little by little up to the dispersion of its parts. It is a loosening that brings to the fore the

---

37. Preface to *Ennead* IV, 3, p. 17.
[The text to which Camus is referring here is Bréhier, *La Philosophie de Plotin*.—Trans.]
38. *Ennead* IV, 3, 4.
39. *Ennead* IV, 3, 8: "Elle est dans tout le corps qu'elle pénètre, par exemple dans chaque partie différente d'une plante, même dans une bouture qu'on en a séparée: elle est à la fois dans la première plante et dans celle qui en est issue par bouture; car le corps de l'ensemble est un corps unique et elle est partout en lui comme un corps unique."
[Plotinus *Ennead* 4.3.8, trans. Armstrong, 61.—Trans.]
40. *Ennead* IV, 4, 3.
[Though Camus' reference implies that this text is taken from the *Enneads*, it actually appears to be from Bréhier, *La Philosophie de Plotin*.—Trans.]
41. *Ennead* IV, 3, 8: "L'une est unie actuellement aux intelligibles, une autre n'y est unie que par la connaissance, une autre par le désir; chacune, contemplant des choses différentes, est et devient ce qu'elle contemple."
[Plotinus *Enneads* 4.3.8, trans. Armstrong, 57.—Trans.]

particularities of individual souls. Plunging into darkness little by little, these souls sink into matter. Here, finally, Plotinian thought is not definitive. For Plotinus, the cause of this fall of the soul is both audacity[42] and blindness.[43] The latter interpretation would seem more orthodox. The soul is reflected in matter, and taking this reflecting for itself, it descends to become united with it, when it should, on the contrary, elevate itself in order to return to its origins.

3) In short, the Plotinian conception of the human soul is closely tied to all that has been said above. The principle that regulates it is this: it is only by its inferior part that the human soul participates in the body. But there is always in it an intelligence directed toward the intelligible world.[44] But constrained to pilot the weak body through the traps of sensible nature, it fails and forgets little by little its princely origin. From this principle follows the whole of Plotinus's psychology. First, if the diversity of souls imitates that of the intelligible world,[45] their function is purely cosmic, and psychology is still physics. Another immediate consequence is that all knowledge that is not intuitive and contemplative participates in the conditions of corporeal life; reasoned thought is only a weakening of intuitive thought. Conscience is an accident and an obsession. Nothing that constitutes it can belong to the superior part of the soul. Memory itself indicates an attachment to sensible forms. The soul, having arrived at the contemplation of intelligibles, will have no memory of its past lives.[46] In this way, there appears a conception of the self, at first sight paradoxical, but very fertile: "There is no point by which it might be able to determine its limits, so as to say: up to that point it is me."[47] We see here the connection between this understanding of the soul and the doctrine of conversion. It is through meditation that the soul forgets practical necessities. By closing its eyes, the sight of Intelligence will be born in it. The desire for God will animate it. It will remount the scale of things and beings. And it will recover the procession through a movement of love—which is conversion.

---

42. *Ennead* IV, 3, 12; IV, 3, 17; IV, 8, 5.
43. *Enneads* IV, 3, 13; VI, 7, 7; V, 2, 7.
44. *Ennead* III, 12, 4, 5.
45. *Ennead* IV, 3, 14.
46. *Ennead* IV, 1, 1, 10.
47. *Ennead* IV, 3, 18 [*sic*]: "Il n'y a pas un point où on puisse fixer ses propres limites, de manière à dire: Jusque-là c'est moi."*

Here are noted, therefore, as briefly as possible, the various stages of the procession. But everything here is not equally satisfying. We have not given an exact reflection of Plotinus's thought. There is no movement in it. We will ask that conversion restore this smooth continuity that leads the soul to the One.

B. *Conversion or the Path of Ecstasy*

It is in the Soul that is found the principle of conversion. The soul is the desire for God and a nostalgia for a lost homeland. Life without God is only a shadow of life. All beings are striving toward God on the ladder of Ideas and attempt to return to the course of the procession. Matter alone, that great indigent, that positive nothing, does not aspire to God, and in it resides the principle of evil: "It is only left for it to be potentially a sort of weak and dim phantasm: so it is actually a falsity: this is the same as that which is truly a falsity'; this is 'what is really unreal.'"[48] But, creator of mirages, it really exists only in the blindness of souls. The principle of conversion finds its source in the Soul and not in matter. But what is this principle? It is the desire for God. And through this desire is revealed the religious aspect of the Hypostases, considered as stages in the Soul's journey in the metaphysical region. "[It has the good sense, then, to remain in itself, and would not come to be in another; but] those other things hang from it as if by their longing they had found where it is. And this is 'Love camping on the doorstep', even coming from outside into the presence of beauty and longing for it, and satisfied if in this way he can have a part in it."[49]

---

48. *Ennead* II, 5, 5: "C'est un fantôme fragile et effacé qui ne peut recevoir une forme. Si elle est en acte, elle est un fantôme en acte, un mensonge en act, c'est-à-dire un mensonge véritable, autant dire le réel non-être."
[Plotinus *Ennead* 2.5.5, trans. Armstrong, 169. Unlike the English translation, Camus' French version of this text does not indicate that the final two phrases of the last sentence are actually quotations from Plato's *Republic* (382a) and *Sophist* (254d), respectively.—Trans.]

49. *Ennead* VI, 5, 10: "Le désir nous fait découvrir l'être universel; ce désir est l'Éros qui veille à la porte de son aimé; toujours dehors et toujours passionné, il se contente d'y participer autant qu'il le peut."
[Plotinus *Ennead* 6.5.10, trans. Armstrong, 349. Again, the English translation of this text, unlike Camus', indicates a quotation from Plato *Symposium* 203c–d.—Trans.]

Desire is in this way frustrated by the world. "So we must 'fly from here' and 'separate' ourselves from what has been added to us."[50] To desire is to love what is absent from us. It is to want to be and to want to be one, because to search for an identity is in a sense to be unified. Beauty itself does not suffice.[51] Thus, virtue is no more than a state that one must pass through in order to reach God.[52] And nothing is desirable except through the One that colors it.[53] The Soul in its wild desire is not content even with Intelligence. "But when a kind of warmth from thence comes upon it, it gains its strength and wakes and is truly winged; and though it is moved with passion for that which lies close by it, yet all the same it rises higher, to something greater which it seems to remember. And as long as there is anything higher than that which is present to it, it naturally goes on upwards, lifted by the giver of its love. It rises above Intellect, but cannot run on above the Good, for there is nothing above. But if it remains in Intellect it sees fair and noble things, but has not yet quite grasped what it is seeking. It is as if it was in the presence of a face which is certainly beautiful, but cannot catch the eye because it has no grace playing upon its beauty."[54]

b) This desire of the Soul contaminates Intelligence. To know is still to desire. To say that Intelligence has need of nothing is to say only that it is independent of the sensible world. But it is turned toward the beyond. It has need of the One. "[Intelligence] lived toward it and depended on it and turned to it."[55] Intelligence lacks something, and

50. *Ennead* II, 3, 9: "Et c'est pourquoi il faut nous enfuir d'ici et nous séparer de ce qui s'est ajouté à nous-même."
[Plotinus *Ennead* 2.3.9, trans. Armstrong, 75. Again the passage includes references to Plato: *Theaetetus* 176a–b and *Phaedo* 67c.—Trans.]

51. *Ennead* V, 5, 12.

52. *Enneads* I, 2, 7; VI, 3, 16; VI, 9, 7.

53. *Ennead* VI, 7, 22.

54. *Ennead* VI, 7, 22. Arnou's translation, *Le Désir de Dieu dans la philosophie de Plotin*, p. 82: "Mais dès que descend sur elle la douce chaleur de là-haut, elle reprend des forces, elle s'éveille en vérité, elle ouvre ses ailes; et tant qu'il y a quelque chose au-dessus de ce qui lui est présent, elle monte naturellement plus haut, attirée par celui qui donne l'amour; elle dépasse l'Intelligence mais ne peut aller au-delà du Bien, car il n'y a rien au-delà. Si elle s'arrête à l'Intelligence, elle voit certes de belles et nobles choses mais elle n'a pas encore tout à fait ce qu'elle cherche. Tel un visage qui, malgré sa beauté ne peut attirer les regards, car il lui manque le reflet de grâce qui est la fleur de la beauté."
[Plotinus *Ennead* 6.7.22, trans. Armstrong, 157.—Trans.]

55. *Ennead* VI, 7, 16: "Elle vit orientée vers lui; elle se suspend à lui; elle se tourne vers lui."
[Plotinus *Ennead* 6.7.16, ibid., 139.—Trans.]

this is its unity. There is in Intelligence an indigence in relation to itself and from which it suffers and stirs. Plotinian Intelligence is not mathematical Reason. Moreover, as we have seen, it is through a return to and contemplation of the One that Intelligence receives its form. This march toward God is for it, therefore, fundamental. And the intelligible world as a whole moves toward the One.

c) But the great problem that conversion evokes is analogous to the one we have found, on three occasions, in the notion of Procession. It is laid out entirely in one text of the *Enneads:* "That which is altogether without a share in the good would not ever seek the good."[56] That is to say: you would not look for me if you had not already found me.[57] Or, in Plotinian terms: desire requires a certain immanence of that which is desired in that which desires. Will the One, then, be transcendent or immanent? This question is much debated, on the one hand by those partisans of Plotinus's pantheism (Zeller), on the other hand, by those who see in the One a doctrine of transcendence (Caird).[58] Without pretending to resolve the question, we can nonetheless attempt to pose it differently.

In our view, God is therefore immanent. Desire demands it. And furthermore, we carry within ourselves the three hypostases, since it is through inner meditation that we attain ecstasy and Union with the One. On the other hand, we cannot deny Plotinus's God an unquestionable transcendence in relation to other beings. When he creates he is not completed but superabounds without being depleted. In order to understand this contradiction, it is necessary to reverse the terms of the problem. If it is true that the one who learns to know himself knows also where he comes from,[59] and if it is true that, being raised to his principle, he is to commune with himself, he must say that God is not immanent in any

---

56. *Ennead* III, 5, 9: "Ce qui n'aurait absolument aucune part au Bien, ne saurait désirer le bien."

[Plotinus *Ennead* 3.5.9, trans. Armstrong, 203.—Trans.]

57. [This is a reference to Pascal's famous remark: "Take comfort; you would not seek me if you had not found me." Blaise Pascal, *Pensées,* trans. A. J. Krailsheimer (London: Penguin Books, 1995), 919 (553).—Trans.]

58. Edward Caird, *The Evolution of Theology in the Greek Philosophers,* vol. 2 (Glasgow: James MacLehose and Sons, 1904), p. 315: "Thus the philosophy of Plotinus is the condemnation of the Greek dualism, just because it is he who carries it to its utmost point."

[In Camus' note, the pages referenced for this quotation are 210 and 393.—Trans.]

59. *Ennead* V, 1, 1.

being, but that all things are immanent to God. "The Soul is not in the universe, but the universe is in it . . . but soul is in Intellect and body in Soul, and Intellect in something else; but there is nothing other than this for it to be in: it is not, then, in anything; in this way therefore, it is nowhere. Where then are the other things? In it."[60] Let us consider, on the other hand, that all being has two actualities: the actuality of essence and an actuality that comes from essence; the former binds it to itself, the latter urges it to create and to leave its own nature. So it is with God. He rises up out of himself, but without failing to keep his essence. The whole error of all overly rigid interpretations of Plotinus is *to place the One in space*. Plotinus's doctrine is an attempt at nonspatial thought. It is on this level, qualitative and inexpressible, that one must attempt to understand it. Or thus, to return to the previous analysis, to a psychological problem: does an abstract thought of space exist, that which is of another order? In attempting to assimilate the Plotinian experience, we see that the first principle is itself present in all Plotinus's works,[61] namely, the principle that the One does not exist locally and that in a certain sense it is both transcendent and immanent to all things.[62] All things considered, it is everywhere on the condition that it is nowhere, because what is bound nowhere has no place where it cannot be.

d) *Ecstasy or Union with the One.* Having examined this problem, we will be able to understand that in order to ascend to God, one must return to oneself. Carrying within itself the reflection of its origins, the

60. *Ennead* V, 5, 9: "L'Ame à son tour n'est pas dans le monde, mais le monde est en elle . . . l'Ame est dans l'Intelligence, le corps est dans l'Ame, l'Intelligence est en un autre principe; mais cet autre principe n'a plus rien de différent où il puisse être: il n'est donc pas en quoi que ce soit et, en ce sens, il n'est nulle part. Où sont donc les autres choses? En lui."

[Plotinus, *Ennead* 5.5.9, trans. Armstrong, 185.—Trans.]

61. Further, cf. *Ennead* VI, 5, 12: "Il n'est pas besoin qu'il vienne pour être présent, c'est vous qui êtes parti; partir ce n'est pas le quitter pour aller ailleurs; car il est là. Mais tout en restant près de lui vous vous en étiez détourné."

[Plotinus *Ennead* 6.5.12: "It did not come in order to be present, but you went away when it was not present. But if you went away, it was not from it—for it is present—and you did not even go away then, but were present and turned the opposite way." *Ennead* 6, trans. Armstrong, 359.—Trans.]

62. On reconciling Christian mysticism. SUSO ex. no. 54: "C'est être en même temps dans toutes choses et en dehors de toutes choses. C'est pourquoi un maître a dit que Dieu est comme un cercle dont le centre est partout et la circonférence nulle part."

["It is to be simultaneously in all things and outside all things. This is why a master has said that God is like a circle of which the center is everywhere and the circumference is nowhere."—Trans.]*

soul must be immersed in God. From God to God, such is its journey;[63] but it must be purified, that is to say, it must be cleansed of what is bound to the soul during generation. It must not cling to what is not the soul,[64] but must return to that homeland,[65] the memory of which occasionally colors our souls' restlessness. The soul, to that end, is destroyed and allows itself to be absorbed into intelligence, which dominates it, and intelligence in its turn endeavors to disappear in order to leave only the One that illuminates it. This union, so complete and so rare,[66] is ecstasy.[67] But here it is up to inner meditation to take over, and Plotinus stops at this point in his journey. The analysis can go no further nor any deeper. This sentiment, so nuanced and so "full" of divinity, this exquisite melancholy of certain Plotinian texts, leads us to the heart of the thought of its author. "Often I have woken up out of the body to my self and have entered into myself."[68] Solitary meditation, in love with the world to the extent that it is only a crystal in which the divinity is reflected, thought wholly penetrated by the silent rhythm of stars, but concerned about the God who orders them, Plotinus thinks as an artist and feels as a philosopher, according to a reason full of light and before a world in which intelligence breathes.

But before bringing into relief the original themes of Plotinus's philosophy, and above all before examining how they serve or disadvantage the evolution of Christian metaphysics, let us consider, according to the texts, what Neoplatonism's attitude was regarding Christianity. We will then have what is necessary in order to judge the originality of Neoplatonism in relation to Christian thought.

---

63. Arnou, [*Le Désir de Dieu,*] 191.

64. *Ennead* V, 5, 8.

65. *Ennead* I, VI, 8.

[In "Summer in Algiers" Camus mentions Plotinus by name and uses his notion of a homeland to explain his own experience of unity with the world. "But at certain moments everything yearns for this homeland of the soul. 'Yes, it is to this we must return.' What is strange about finding on earth the unity Plotinus longed for?" Camus, "Summer in Algiers," in *Lyrical and Critical Essays,* ed. Philip Thody, trans. Ellen Conroy Kennedy (New York: Knopf, 1968), 90. The notions of exile and homeland later became important images in the iconography of Camus' work and in his critical assessment of modernity.—Trans.]

66. Porphyry, *Vie de Plotin,* 23.

[*The Life of Plotinus.*—Trans.]

67. Principal texts: *Enneads* IV, 8, 1; VI, 9, 9; VI, 7, 39; VI, 8, 19.

68. *Ennead* IV, 8, 1: "Souvent je m'éveille à moi-même en m'échappant de mon corps." [Plotinus *Ennead* 4.8.1, trans. Armstrong, 397.—Trans.]

II. The Resistance

The fervor with which Plotinus ascends toward God could delude us and tempt us to believe him more Christian than he was capable of being. His attitude toward the Gnostics, that is to say, regarding a certain form of Christian thought, and the more categorical position of his disciple Porphyry, will permit us, on the contrary, to judge prudently.

a) It is in the ninth treatise of *Ennead* II that Plotinus writes against a Gnostic sect that has yet to be defined precisely.[69] There he contrasts eloquently his own coherent and harmonious universe with the romantic universe of the Gnostics. Through this contrast, we can grasp instantly a certain number of insurmountable oppositions between them. Plotinus's reproaches bear on roughly four points, of varying importance moreover. He reproaches the Gnostics for despising the created world and for believing that a new world awaits them,[70] for believing themselves to be children of God and for substituting for universal harmony a providence that will satisfy their egoism,[71] for calling the most vile men brothers, even though they do not accord this name to the gods,[72] and for having substituted for the virtue of wisdom the idea of an arbitrary salvation in which man has no part.[73]

This treatise is actually entitled "Against those who say that the demiurge of the world is wicked and that the world is evil." At bottom it is the æsthetic point of view that is taken here: "The whole heaven and the stars there have no share given them in the immortal soul, though they are made of much fairer and purer material, though these people see the order there and the excellence of form and arrangement, and are particularly addicted to complaining about the disorder here around the earth!"[74] And further on: "Again, despising the

---

69. Perhaps a sect of the Followers of the Mother: *Ennead* II, 9, 10; II, 9, 12.

70. *Ennead* II, 9, 5.

71. *Ennead* II, 9, 9.

72. *Ennead* II, 9, 18.

73. *Ennead* II, 9, 15.

74. *Ennead* II, 9, 5: "Le ciel est fait pourtant de choses bien plus belles et bien plus pures que notre corps: ils en voient la régularité, la belle ordonnance et ils blâment plus que personne le désordre des choses terrestres." Cf. above all *Ennead* II, 9, 17: "Il n'est pas possible qu'un être réellement beau à l'extérieur ait une âme laide."

[Plotinus *Ennead* 2.9.5, ibid., 239. *Ennead* 2.9.17: "But perhaps it is not really possible for anything to be beautiful outwardly but ugly inwardly" (ibid., 295).—Trans.]

universe and the gods in it and other noble things is certainly not becoming good."[75]

b) It is therefore through his sense of the order and economy of the world that Plotinus feels himself wounded. "Then besides this, God in his providence cares for you; why does he neglect the whole universe in which you yourselves are? . . . But they have no need of him. But the universe does need him, and knows its station."[76] Dramatic climaxes, creation, this human and sensible god, all this is repugnant to Plotinus. But perhaps even more repugnant to him—to his aristocracy—is the unrealistic Christian humanitarianism: "Do the Gnostics think it right to call the lowest of men brothers, but refuse, in their 'raving talk,' to call the sun and the gods in the sky brothers and the soul of the universe sister?"[77] It is, therefore, also ancient Greek naturalism that protests in Plotinus.

But it is very certain that all these objections are summed up in Greek wisdom's revulsion regarding Christian "anarchy." The theory of unmerited and irrational Salvation is at bottom the object of all the attacks of this treatise. As we have seen, this doctrine of salvation implies a certain disinterest regarding virtue in the Hellenic sense. To appeal to God, to believe in him and to love him, atones thoroughly for one's errors. Plotinus has well understood to criticize precisely this point, and he did so with uncommon violence: "This, too, is evidence of their indifference to virtue, that they have never made any treatise about virtue . . . For it does no good at all to say 'Look to God,' unless one also teaches how one is to look. In reality it is virtue which goes before us to the good and, when it comes to exist in the soul along with wisdom, shows God; but God, if you talk about him without true virtue, is only a name."[78]

75. *Ennead* II, 9, 16: "Non, encore une fois, mépriser le monde, mépriser les dieux et toutes les beautés qui sont en lui ce n'est pas devenir un homme de bien."
[Plotinus *Ennead* 2.9.16, ibid., 285.—Trans.]
76. *Ennead* II, 9, 9: "Si Dieu exerce sa providence en votre faveur, pourquoi négligerait-il l'ensemble du monde dans lequel vous êtes . . . les hommes, dites-vous, n'ont pas besoin qu'il regarde le monde. Oui, mais le monde en a besoin. Ainsi le monde connaît son ordre propre."
[Plotinus *Ennead* 2.9.9, ibid., 261–63.—Trans.]
77. *Ennead* II, 9, 18: "Voilà des gens qui ne dédaignent pas de donner le nom de frères aux hommes les plus vils; mais ils ne daignent accorder ce nom au soleil, aux astres du ciel et pas même à l'aimé du monde tellement leur langage s'égare."
[Plotinus *Ennead* 2.9.18, ibid., 297–99.—Trans.]
78. *Ennead* II, 9, 15: "Ce qui prouve ce défaut [méconnaissance de la nature divine]

The arbitrariness inherent in any doctrine of salvation cannot be reconciled with a doctrine in which beings act according to the necessities of their nature, and not, as Plotinus becomes indignant about it, at one moment rather than at another.[79]

It must be well understood that it is a matter of Gnosticism and that these reproaches are addressed to a certain caricature of Christianity. But in the end, Plotinus is fighting far more an attitude toward the world than the details of doctrine. In this sense, what are opposed are two reflections on the human condition. We already know enough about these reflections to determine how, on certain points, they remain irreconcilable.

Plotinus's disciple, however, has gone further and has not hesitated to write an entire work against the Christians. It took him between 35 and 40 years to write it (after 208 CE). This treatise was composed of no less than fifteen books. We know his work through the fragments[80] gathered by Harnack. We will leave aside the detailed critiques (implausibility, contradiction) that Porphyry does not fail to formulate. They constitute the common foundation of all pagan polemical works. We will cite only those texts that contrast, on points of doctrine, Christianity and Neoplatonism.

Porphyry complains that the apostles had been unintelligent peasants.[81] The complaint is common, but further on he reproaches the believers for being attached to an "irrational faith"[82] and expresses himself in these terms: "The great work of Christ on this earth is to have concealed from the wise the ray of science in order to reveal it to beings deprived of sense and to unweaned infants."[83]

chez eux, c'est qu'ils n'ont aucune doctrine de la vertu. Il est tout é fait superflu de dire: Regardez vers Dieu, si l'on n'enseigne pas comment regarder. Ce sont les progrès de la vertu intérieure à l'âme et accompagnée de prudence qui nous font voir Dieu. Sans la vertu véritable, Dieu n'est qu'un mot."
    [Plotinus *Ennead* 2.9.15, ibid., 285.—Trans.]
    79. *Ennead* II, 9, 4; II, 9, 11.
    80. Saint Jerome, *Chronique d'Eusèbe: Manuscrit de Macarius.*
    [The English title of Jerome's work is *Eusebius's Chronicle. Manuscrit de Macarius* appears to refer to a later edition of Jerome's collected works by Marianus Victorius.—Trans.]
    81. Fragment 4, cited by De Labriolle, *La Réaction païenne,* p. 256.
    82. Fragment 73, according to De Labriolle, [*La Réaction païenne,*] p. 212 [*sic*]: "Foi irrationnelle."*
    [The page reference in Labriolle should be p. 272.—Trans.]
    83. Fragment 52 according to Labriolle, [*La Réaction païenne,*] p. 272: "La grande trouvaille du Christ sur cette terre c'est d'avoir dissimulé aux sages le rayon de la science pour le dévoiler aux êtres privés de sens et aux nourrissons."*

Regarding his understanding of the Christian conception of the world, Porphyry stumbles upon this Pauline text: "The form of this world is passing away."[84] How could the world pass away, asks Porphyry, and what could make it pass away: "If it had been the demiurge, he would expose himself to the reproach of disturbing and distorting a peacefully established whole . . . If the condition of this world is truly dismal, a concert of protests should rise up against the demiurge for having arranged the elements of the Universe in such a deplorable way, in disregard for the rational character of nature."[85]

Christian eschatology offends, not only Porphyry's idea of order, but also his æsthetic sense: "And he, the Creator, he would see heaven (can we imagine something more wonderfully beautiful than heaven?) dissolve, whereas the decayed, destroyed bodies of men would rise from the dead, among them those who, before death, presented a hard and repulsive aspect."[86]

Moreover, Porphyry occasionally passes from indignation over into insult.[87] A cultivated Greek could not adopt this attitude without serious reasons.

III. The Meaning and Influence of Neoplatonism

But it is time to determine the meaning of the Neoplatonic solution and its role in the evolution of Christian metaphysics. Our task here will

---

[The text in English translation that most closely approximates the one Camus cites is as follows: "He thanked his Father that these things were revealed unto babes. If so, they certainly ought to have been spoken more plainly. If his object was to hide them from the wise, and reveal them to fools, it must be better to seek after ignorance than knowledge." T. W. Crafer, "The Work of Porphyry against the Christians, and Its Reconstruction," *Journal of Theological Studies* 15 (1913–1914): 504.—Trans.]

84. 1 Corinthians 7:31.

85. Fragment 34, according to Labriolle, [*La Réaction païenne,*] p. 260: "Si c'était le démiurge un ensemble paisiblement établi . . . Si vraiment la condition du monde est lugubre, c'est un concert de protestations qui doit s'élever contre le démiurge, pour avoir disposé les éléments de l'Univers d'une façon si fâcheuse au mépris du caractère rationnel de la nature."*

86. Fragment 94, according to Labriolle, [*La Réaction païenne,*] p. 287: "Et lui, le Créateur, il verrait le ciel (peut-on imaginer quelque chose de plus admirablement beau que le ciel) se liquéfier . . . tandis que les corps pourris, anéantis des hommes ressusciteraient, y compris ceux qui avant la mort offraient un aspect pénible et repoussant."*

87. Fragments 23, 35, 49, 54, 55, according to Labriolle, [*La Réaction païenne,*] p. 287.

be to bring out the novelty of Neoplatonism and to indicate in what directions it has exercised its influence. Our study of Christianity will permit us to enter into the detail of this influence. But let us first summarize in a few words the general characteristics of Neoplatonism.

a) It is a never-ending task to reconcile contradictory notions with the assistance of a principle of participation, which is valid only in nonspatial and nontemporal logic. Mystic reason, sensible Intelligence, God, who is both immanent and transcendent, such contradictions abound. However, they all indicate a constant movement between the sensible and the intellectual, between the religious aspect of principles and their explanatory power. In this dialogue between the heart and Reason, truth can only be expressed through images. This is the source of the abundance of comparisons in Plotinus. This wealth of images doubtless corresponds to the same need as did the Evangelical parables: to cast the intelligible in a sensible form, rendering to intuition what would belong to Reason. But at the same time, these apparent contradictions are clarified through the hypothesis of a form of thought situated outside Space and Time. This is why Plotinus's originality resides above all in the method that governs his reconciliations. But a method is valuable only to the extent that it expresses a need in the nature of its author. We have also shown that this was the case with Plotinus.

What place must we attribute, therefore, to Neoplatonism between Hellenism and Christianity? Regarding the former, we have sufficiently demonstrated that the *Enneads* contain what is purely Hellenic. But something nevertheless made Plotinus a completely original figure. In Plato's writings, myths of the destiny of the soul seem added and juxtaposed to properly rational explanations. In Plotinus, the two processes form one body, and neither can be excluded, since they conceal the same reality. This is the difference essential to understand and which distinguishes Plotinus in his epoch. It is a difference equally valuable with regard to Christianity, since, all the more, it is the rational aspect that is missing from Christian thought. Midway between two doctrines,[88] Plotinus is clearly appointed to serve as intercessor.

b) To tell the truth, what Neoplatonism has furnished Christianity with for its subsequent development is a method and a direction of thought.

---

88. Here would be placed the question of Plotinus's Orientalism.

We say a direction of thought because, in furnishing Christianity with ready-made structures for religious thoughts, Neoplatonism necessarily oriented it toward the ways of looking inward from which these structures had been created. It is toward the reconciliation of metaphysics and primitive faith that Alexandrian thought encouraged Christianity to move. But here there was little to do—the movement was given. The method, however, arrived at the right moment. It is actually according to the principle of participation that Christianity will resolve its great problems, that is to say, the problems of the Incarnation and the Trinity. But let us attempt to clarify this by means of a specific example.

Arius[89] relied on certain scriptural texts in order to affirm the creation of the Son by the Father and the subordination of the one to the other. "The Lord has created me to be the beginning of his ways."[90]

Neither the Angels in Heaven nor the Son are informed about the day or the hour. Only the Father knows them. Then Arius cited Johannine texts. "[If you loved me, you would have rejoiced,] because I go to the Father; for the Father is greater than I."[91] "And this is eternal life, that they know thee the only true God, and Jesus Christ whom thou hast sent."[92] "The Son can do nothing of his own accord."[93]

To this affirmation, Athanasius, defender of orthodoxy, opposed three explicit texts by John: "I and the Father are one."[94] "The Father is in me and I am in the Father."[95] "He who sees me sees him who sent me."[96] According to these texts, the Son was and was not God. But Neoplatonism's classic question is: who sees only the problem posed in this manner? And how can one be surprised if it is according to a similar method that Christian thought will bring the debate to a close? The Nicean symbol (325 CE) established the principle of consubstantiality

---

89. For the history of Arianism, cf. Tixeront, *Histoire des dogmes dans l'antiquité chrétienne*, vol. II, chap. II.

90. VIII, 22.

[Camus does not indicate the text from which this passage is cited. The text which most closely approximates it, in terms of its content, is Luke 1:76b: "For you will go before the Lord to prepare his ways."—Trans.]

91. John 14:28.

92. John 17:3.

93. John 5:19; also John 11:33, 38; Luke 2:52; Matthew 26:39; Philemon 19; Hebrews 1:9.

94. John 10:30.

95. John 10:38.

96. John 12:45.

and opposed the begotten Christ to the Jesus created by Arius. "We believe in One God, Father Almighty, the Maker of all things visible and invisible. And in One Lord Jesus Christ, the Word of God, God from God, Light from Light, Life from Life, Only-begotten Son, first-born of all creation, before all the ages begotten from the Father, by Whom also all things were made; Who for our salvation was incarnated, and lived among men, and suffered, and rose again on the third day, and ascended to the Father, and will come again in glory to judge living and dead. And we believe also in One Holy Spirit."[97] And if this text does not seem sufficiently explicit, consider Athanasius's *Defense of the Nicene Council,* in which he cites Theognoste, head of the Catechetical School of Alexandria between 270 and 280 CE.[98] "The essence of the Son is not procured from without, nor accruing out of nothing, but it sprang from the Father's essence, as the radiance of light, as the vapour of water; for neither the radiance, nor the vapour, is the water itself or the sun itself, nor is it alien; but it is an effluence of the Father's essence, which, however, suffers no partition. For as the sun remains the same, and is not impaired by the rays poured forth by it, so neither does the Father's essence suffer any change, though it has the Son as an Image of Itself."[99]

These texts are significant and show us the nature of Neoplatonism's influence concerning methods of resolution. Numerous texts might further demonstrate it.[100] But as eloquent as these reconciliations may be,

---

97. In Hésèle, *Histoire des Conciles,* vol. I, pp. 443, 444: "Nous croyons en un seul Dieu, Père tout-puissant, créateur des choses visibles et invisibles et en un Seigneur Jésus-Christ, fils de Dieu, lumière des lumières, vrai Dieu, engendré, non créé, de la même substance que le Père, par qui toutes choses ont été engendrées et celles qui sont dans le ciel pour nous et notre salut, s'est fait homme, a souffert, est ressuscité le troisième jour, est monté aux cieux, et il viendra juger les vivants et les morts. Et au Saint Esprit."
[Cited in *A New Eusebius,* ed. J. Stevenson (London: S. P. C. K., 1957), 364.—Trans.]
98. Plotinus died in 270.
[Notes 253 and 254 (notes 97 and 98 herein) have been reversed in my translation in order to clarify the references.—Trans.]
99. No. 25 [*sic*]: "La substance du Fils n'est pas venue du dehors, elle n'a pas été tirée du néant, elle provient de la substance du Père comme l'éclat provient de la lumière, la vapeur de l'eau, car la splendeur n'est pas le soleil même, la vapeur n'est pas l'eau même. Ce n'est pas cependant une chose étrangère, c'est une émanation de la substance du Père, sans que celle-ci subisse aucune division. De même que le soleil demeurant ce qu'il est n'est pas diminué par les rayons qu'il répand; de même la substance du Père ne subit aucune altération en ayant son fils pour image."
[Athanasius, *Defense of the Nicene Council,* ch. 6, section 25, trans. Newman, in *The Nicene and Post Nicene Fathers,* vol. 4, ed. A. Robertson (Grand Rapids: Wm. B. Eerdmans, 1966), 166–67.—Trans.]
100. Saint Basil, *Homélies sur le précepte "Observation,"* par. 7, et Eusèbe de Césarée,

let us not draw from them hasty or overly generous conclusions regarding Neoplatonism. Christianity lies elsewhere, and with it its fundamental originality.

c) We see therefore in what sense we can speak of Neoplatonism's influence on Christian thought. To tell the truth, it is the influence of a metaphysical doctrine on a religious form of thought: this is what Neoplatonism provides for Christianity. It is therefore with good reason that we have taken Plotinus's thought as the symbol of this influence. It has prepared and made more flexible formulas which, in the required time, were ready to be used by Christianity. Apart from that which is moving and original in itself, its role stops there. Too many things separate Saint Augustine and Plotinus.

Préparat. Évang. XII, 17 [*sic*]: "C'est le rayonnement d'une lumière qui s'en échappe sans troubler sa quiétude, etc."

[Eusebius, *Preparation for the Gospel*, 11.17, trans. E. H. Gifford (Oxford: Clarendon Press, 1903), pt. 2, p. 577: "[How then and what must we conceive concerning that abiding substance?] A light shining around and proceeding from it, while it remains itself unchanged."—Trans.]

Chapter Four

Augustine

I. The Second Revelation

A. *The Psychological Experience of Saint Augustine and Neoplatonism*

a) Before demonstrating how the evolution that we have attempted to retrace finds in Augustinianism one of its most admirable formulas, it is necessary for us to consider the Neoplatonism of Saint Augustine. Let us first state the problem: the new Platonic philosophy has exercised its influence over the great doctor. He cites several texts of the *Enneads*.[1] We can compare a certain number of Augustinian texts and Plotinian thoughts. The most suggestive in this regard concern the nature of God.

On God's ineffability: *Sermon* 117, 5; *De civitate Dei* IX, 16 with *Enneads* VI, 9, 5; *De Trinitate*, VIII, 2 and XV, 5 with *Enneads* V, 3, 13; on his eternity: *Confessions* XI, 13 and *Enneads* III, 6, 7; on his ubiquity: *Sermon* 277, 13 and 18 with *Enneads* VI, 4, 2; on his spirituality: *De civitate Dei* XIII, 5 and *Enneads* VI, 8, 11. From this influence some have

---

1. *Enneads* I, 5, *On Beauty;* III, 6, [*sic*] *On Providence;* III, 4, *On Our Allotted Guardian Spirit;* IV, 3, *On Difficulties about the Soul;* VI, [*sic*] *On the Three Primary Hypostases;* V, 6, *On the Fact that That Which is beyond Being Does Not Think.*

[The reference for *On Providence* should be 3.2, 3, and for *On the Three Primary Hypostases*, 5.1.—Trans.]

been able to draw excessive conclusions.[2] However, Saint Augustine's testimony is sufficiently explicit. And the celebrated passage of the *Confessions* on the "books of the Platonists" gives us a very clear account of the question. Despite its length, permit us to quote the passage in full. Everything that follows will be instructive for us: "I read . . . that at the Beginning of time the Word already was; and God had the Word abiding with him, and the Word was God . . . [and that] the Word, who is himself God, is the true Light, which enlightens every soul born into the world . . .

"But I did not read in them that the Word was made flesh and came to dwell among us . . . [and] they do not say that he dispossessed himself, and took on the nature of a slave, fashioned in the likeness of men, and presenting himself to us in human form; and then he lowered his own dignity, accepted an obedience that brought him to death."[3] Opposing Incarnation to Contemplation, Saint Augustine had clarified for the first time the oppositions and similarities between these two forms of thought.

b) But at least how far does this influence reach? What is striking in Augustinian thought is that it gathers, in a few years,[4] the hesitations and reversals of Christian thought. Highly passionate, sensual, the fear of not being able to maintain continence, all these delay Augustine's conversion for a long time.[5] But he also has a taste for rational truths. It is this concern for reason that leads him to adhere to Manichaeanism, and even to Carthage, in the midst of an exuberant and voluptuous life.[6]

---

2. Alfaric, *L'Évolution intellectuelle de Saint Augustin.*

3. *Confessions* VIII, C, IX: "Je lus . . . que le verbe était dès le commencement; que le verbe était en Dieu et que le verbe était Dieu; qu'aussi dès le commencement le verbe était Dieu . . . que le verbe de Dieu, qui est Dieu, est cette lumière véritable qui illumine tout homme venant en ce monde . . . Mais je n'y lus pas le verbe a été fait homme et a habité parmi nous . . . mais je n'y lus pas qu'il s'est anéanti soi-même en prenant la forme d'un esclave; qu'il se soit rendu semblable à l'homme en se revêtant de ses informités; qu'il s'est humilié et a été obéissant jusqu'à la mort."

[Saint Augustine, *Confessions*, 7.9, trans. R. S. Pine-Coffin (Baltimore: Penguin Books, 1961), 144–45.—Trans.]

4. 354, 430.

5. *Confessions* VIII, ch. 1: "Adhuc tenaciter colligabar ex femina."

[Saint Augustine, *Confessions*, bk. 8, ch. 1: "I was still held firm in the bonds of woman's love," ibid., 158.—Trans.]

6. Cf. Salvian, *De Gubernatore Dei, Patrologie Latine*, VII, 16–17: "Débordants de vices, bouillonnants d'iniquité, des hommes engourdis par le vice et enflés de nourriture puaient la sale volupté."

On many points, Manichaeanism merely continued Gnosticism, but it promised demonstrations. This is what attracted Saint Augustine.[7]

But the problem of evil obsessed him as well: "I was still trying to discover the origin of evil, and I could find no solution."[8] And he is haunted by the idea of death.

"[These were the thoughts which I turned over and over in my unhappy mind,] and my anxiety was all the more galling for the fear that death might come before I had found the truth."[9] Greek in his need for coherence, Christian in the anxieties of his sensitivity, for a long time he remained on the periphery of Christianity. It was both the allegorical method of Saint Ambrose and Neoplatonic thought that convinced Saint Augustine. But at the same time they did not persuade him. The conversion was delayed. From this it appeared to him that above all the solution was not in knowledge, that the way out of his doubts and his disgust for the flesh was not through intellectual escapism, but through a full awareness of his depravity and his misery. To love these possessions that carried him so low: grace would raise him high above them.

Saint Augustine found himself therefore at the crossroads of the influences that we are here attempting to determine. But what is the precise extent of these influences? This is what must be defined.

c) What Saint Augustine demanded beside faith was truth, and beside dogmas, metaphysics. And through Augustine, Christianity itself demanded it. But if one moment he adopts Neoplatonism, this was in

---

[Salvian, *On the Government of God*, bk. 7, ch. 16, trans. E. M. Sanford (New York: Octagon Books, 1966), 211: "[For I see the city] overflowing with vice, boiling over with every sort of iniquity—full indeed of people, but even fuller of dishonor, full of riches but fuller still of vice." Camus' reference should be *De Gubernatione Dei, Patrologia Latina*. It seems odd that Camus would offer a French translation of this passage when he claims to be citing a Latin text.—Trans.]

7. *Confessions* VII, 67, 24. Tes. col. 739 [*sic*]: "Il me persuadait que je devais me fier à des maîtres qui m'instruiraient plutôt qu'à ceux qui procéderaient par autorité."

[Saint Augustine, *Confessions*: "He persuaded me that I must have confidence in the masters who instruct me rather than in those who would proceed by authority."—Trans.]*

8. *De Beata vita* 4 [*sic*]: "Je cherchais d'où vient la mal et je n'en sortais pas."

[Saint Augustine, *Confessions*, 7.7, trans. Pine-Coffin, 142. Nowhere in *De Beata Vita* have I been able to find the remark Camus cites. The passage I have offered in its place is found in the *Confessions*, which seems to be its real source.—Trans.]

9. *Confessions* LVII, col. 152 [*sic*], *Patrologia Latina*, vol. 33, col. 737: "J'étais rongé par la crainte de mourir sans avoir découvert la vérité." Cf. also his fear of death: *Confessions* VI, 16; VII, 19–26; *Soliloquia* I, 16; II, 1.

[Saint Augustine, *Confessions*, 7.5, trans. Pine-Coffin, 139.—Trans.]

order soon to transfigure it. And through Augustine, Christianity itself demanded it.[10] Our task is to clarify the meaning of this transfiguration. As we have seen, Plotinus provides Saint Augustine with a doctrine of the intermediate word and, what is more, a solution to the problem of evil.

The hypostasized intelligence actually clarifies the destiny of Christ as the word of God. "We have learned from a divine source that the Son of God is none other than the Wisdom of God—and most certainly the Son of God is God . . . but what do you think the wisdom of God is if not truth. And indeed, it has been said: I am the truth" (*De Beata Vita,* ch. IV, no. 34, P.L.I. 32, col. 975). As for evil, Plotinianism teaches Augustine that it is tied to matter and that its reality is entirely negative (*Conf.* VII, 12, VIII, 13). And by this all Saint Augustine's doubts seem to have vanished. But for all that, conversion did not come. There is this curiosity about the author of the *Confessions,* namely, that his experience remains the perpetual reference for his intellectual pursuits. Satisfied but unconvinced, he himself remarks that it is the Incarnation and its humility that Neoplatonism has been unable to offer to him. Only after having understood this did an outburst of tears and joy come to deliver him in the garden of his home. It was virtually a physical conversion, so total that Saint Augustine moves progressively toward renouncing all that was his life and to consecrating himself to God.

It is therefore this place, given to Christ and the Incarnation in Christianity's originality, that one must note in Augustine. These are the formulas and themes that he asked of Neoplatonism. The figure of Jesus and the problem of Redemption will transfigure everything. It is this conjunction of Greek themes and Christian dogmas that we must attempt to examine in a few points of Augustine's doctrine.

B. *Hellenism and Christianity in Saint Augustine*

1) *Evil, Grace and Freedom.* In the examination of such specifically Christian problems, our constant task will be to bring to light, in

---

10. J. Martin, *Philon,* 1907, p. 67: "After St. Paul, the fathers naturally had to adopt the language that Greek and Alexandrian speculation had created; and by means of this language they expressed the truths that neither Philo nor any Alexandrian had conceived"; and Puech, *Les Apologistes grecs du IIe siècle de notre ère:* "The essential fact is that in principle, the doctrine of the Apologists is religious and not philosophical; they believe first of all in Jesus, the Son of God. And they thus understand his divinity by the pre-existence

Augustinianism, the fundamental themes of Christianity. To tell the truth, a simple reminder will suffice, since we have already studied these themes.

a) We will not go back over the importance that the problem of evil assumes for Saint Augustine. However, it is necessary to note the extreme fecundity of this obsession. It is by beginning from this point that our author has been able to develop his most original doctrines. This same wealth will force us to divide our material. On the one hand, Saint Augustine's thought is maintained doctrinally; on the other, in reaction to Pelagius. Let us examine first his general doctrine, and then the controversy with the Pelagians will clarify, under the harsher light of polemics, the profound tendencies of Augustinianism.

Neoplatonism maintains that evil is a privation and not a true reality. Saint Augustine agrees with this view.[11] But still it is necessary to distinguish two types of evil: natural evil (the misery of our condition, the tragedy of human destinies) and moral evil, that is to say, Sin. The former is explained to the extent that shadows are justified in a painting.[12] It serves the universal harmony. Concerning the latter type, the question is more complex. How is it possible that God has endowed us with free will, that is to say, a will capable of doing evil: "Because [man] is what he now is, he is not good, nor is it in his power to become good, either because he does not see what he ought to be, or, seeing it, has not the power to be what he sees he ought to be."[13] It is that sin, the consequence of original sin, is attributable to us. God has given us the free will of Adam, but our will has acquired the desire to serve evil. And we are so profoundly corrupted that it is from God alone that comes all good use of free will. Left to himself, man would possess in himself only wickedness,

---

of the word." And finally Le Breton, *Les Origines du Dogme de la Trinité,* 1910, p. 521: "If the Theology of the Logos appeared to be so profoundly transformed, it is because the person of Jesus to whom it had been applied imposed upon it these transformations."

11. *De Natura Boni* IV, P.L. vol. 42, col. 553.

[The full title of this work is *De Natura Boni Contra Manichaeos.*—Trans.]

12. *Contre Julianum* 111, 206, P.L. 45, col. 334.

[The text to which Camus is referring is not Augustine's *Contra Iulianum* but rather his *Contra secundam Iuliani responsionem imperfectum* 111, 206, P.L. 45, col. 1334.—Trans.]

13. *De libero arbitrio* L 3, chap. 18, no. 51, P.L. 32–1268.

[Saint Augustine, *On Free Will,* 3.51, in *The Library of Christian Classics,* vol. 6, ed. J. Ballie and J. T. McNeill, trans. J. H. S. Burleigh (Philadelphia: Westminster Press, 1969), 201.—Trans.]

falsehood, and sin: "No one has anything of his own except falsehood and sin."[14] It is God who restores him when he deigns to do so. This is why the virtues that reside in us only have meaning and value through God's assistance, special and suited to our weakness; namely, through his grace. Saint Augustine lays great stress upon the vanity of virtue itself. First grace, then virtue; here we recognize an Evangelical theme.

Thus it is that pagan virtues are ineffectual. God has given them virtues in order to urge us to acquire them if we lack them, and to humble our pride if we possess them. In Christianity, virtue, in the Hellenic sense, was never so severely tried and never on such frequent occasions.[15] Moreover, these natural virtues instead become vices when man glorifies himself through them.[16] Pride is the sin of Satan. On the contrary, our only legitimate end is God. And the gift God makes of his grace is always the result of his generosity. This grace is free. Those who believe they can acquire it through good works take things the wrong way. Grace would not be free if it were possible to merit it. It is necessary to go even further. To believe in God is already to experience his grace. Faith begins with Grace.[17]

We see to what extremes Augustine can go in his thinking. He never spares himself any of the problem's difficulty. Of course, there is still no problem where there is only submission. Nevertheless, as is the rule in what concerns evil, this absolute dependence gives rise to great difficulties. Here divine grace is absolutely arbitrary: man must only have faith in God. How then can we speak of human freedom? But the difficulty is that our only freedom is precisely the freedom to do evil.[18] Saint

---

14. In *Johann.* V, 1 [*sic*], P.L. 18, vol. 35, col. 414: "Nemo habet de suo nisi mendacium atque peccatum." Also, *Sermones* 156, II, 12; P.L. vol. 38, col. 856: "Cumdico tibi: Sine adjutorio Dei nihil agis nihil boni dico, nam ad male agendum habes sine adjutorio Dei liberam voluntatem."

[Saint Augustine, *Homilies on the Gospel of John*, 5.1, in *The Nicene and Post-Nicene Fathers*, vol. 7, ed. P. Schaff, trans. J. Gibb and J. Innes (Grand Rapids: Wm. B. Eerdmans, 1956), 31. The full Latin title of this work is *Ioannis Evangelium.*—Trans.]

15. *De civitate Dei* V, 18, 3, P.L. vol. 41, col. 165 [*sic*]; V, 19, P.L. vol. 41, col. 165–66; *Epistolae* 138, II, 17, P.L. vol. 33, col. 33; *De Patientia* XXVII, 25, P.L. vol. 40, col. 624. *De gratia Christi* XXIV, 25, P.L. vol. 44, col. 376.

16. *De civitate Dei* XXI, 16, P. L., vol. 41, col. 730, and XIX, chap. 25, untitled: "Quod non possint ibi verae esse virtutes ubi non est vera religio" (vol. 41, col. 656). Cf. also *De diversis quaestionibus* 83, 66, P.L. vol. 40, col. 63.

17. Above all *De diversis quaestionibus* bk. I, 2, P.L. vol. 40, col. 111.

18. On the metaphysical plane. In psychology, Saint Augustine concedes free will.

Augustine's final word on this question, vital for a Christian, is an admission of ignorance. Divine arbitrariness remains intact.[19]

It is this theory that Saint Augustine has been led to develop in all its detail in the face of the Pelagian heresy. In this case, he has been able to surpass his own thought for the needs of the cause. But it is also that his pessimism and his renunciation have retained all their bitterness. It is in this way, then, that his doctrine of freedom takes shape.

b) The fierceness that Saint Augustine puts into his fight against Pelagianism will be explained if we summarize the latter's thought.[20] It is from his profound experience, from his acute awareness of the wickedness in man, that Saint Augustine was suffering.

A Breton monk, Pelagius feared at bottom a certain complacency in sin that can be drawn from the doctrine of predestination. A man of conscience rather than of ideas, these especially are his disciples: Celestius and Julian, who propagate his doctrines.

According to Pelagius, man had been created free. He can do good or evil as he pleases. This freedom is an emancipation from God. "Freedom of will, whereby a man was emancipated from God, consists of the ability to commit sin or refrain from sin."[21]

The loss of this freedom was for Saint Augustine a consequence of original sin. On the contrary, the Pelagians thought that Freedom, being governed entirely by the will, implies that man could, if he desired it, avoid sin. "I say that it is possible for a man to be without sin."[22]

---

19. *De diversis quaestionibus* I, 2, 16, P.L. vol. 40, cols. 120, 121.

20. For the works of Pelagius (*Commentarium in Epistulas Sancti Pauli; Epistula ad Demetriadem; Libellus Fidei ad Innocentium papam*) and those of Julian and Celestius, see P.L. vol. 30.

21. Julian, according to Augustine, *Contra Iulianum* I, 78, P.L. vol. 45, col. 1101. See also Pelagius, *Libellus Fidei* 13.

["Libertas arbitri qua a Deo emancipatus homo est, in admittendi peccati et abstinendi a peccato possibilitate consistit [*sic*]." This passage is not from Augustine's *Contra Iulianum*, as Camus suggests, but rather from his *Contra secundam Iuliani responsionem imperfectum* 1.78. The passage should read: "Libertas arbitrii, qua a Deo emancipatus homo est, in admittendi peccati et abstinendi a peccato possibilitate consistit." There is no standard English translation of this text. The English translation I offer here is by Guy Chamberland, Laurentian University.—Trans.]

22. Pelagius, according to Augustine, *De natura et Gratia.* Cf. also *De Gratia Christi* I, 5, and *De gestis Pelagii.*

["Ego dico posses esse hominem sine peccato." Saint Augustine, *On Nature and Grace* 8, in *The Nicene and Post-Nicene Fathers*, ed. P. Schaff, trans. P. Holmes and R. E. Wallis (Grand Rapids: Wm. B. Eerdmans, 1956), 123.—Trans.]

But then the doctrine of original sin loses all significance. And the Pelagians reject this doctrine absolutely as leading to Manichean conclusions. If Adam has injured us, it is only through his poor example. We must not even accept the secondary consequences of the fall, like the loss of the soul's immortality. According to Pelagius, Adam was born a mortal. Nothing of his error has been passed on to us. "New-born infants are in the same condition as Adam was before the fall."[23]

If we sin easily, it is because sin has become in us a second nature.[24] As the Pelagians see it, and strictly speaking, grace is useless. But as always according to Pelagius, creation is already a form of grace. For all that, grace retains its usefulness not "in order to accomplish" but "in order to accomplish more easily [the works of God]."[25] It is an aid, a recommendation with which God provides us.

This doctrine is found summarized in the nine points of accusation accepted by the Council of Carthage (April 29, 418).[26] In a general way, it demonstrates confidence in man and rejects explanations by divine arbitrariness. It is also an act of faith in man's nature and independence. So many things that should make a man indignant fill the cry of Saint Paul: "Wretched man that I am! Who will deliver me from this body of death?"[27] But graver consequences followed from this. The fall denied, Redemption lost its meaning. Grace was a pardon and not a type of protection. Above all, this was to declare the independence of man in relation to God and to deny that constant need of the creator that is at the heart of the Christian religion.

Against this doctrine, Saint Augustine concluded his theories with a certain number of affirmations. Adam possessed immortality.[28] He was free in that he had the "ability not to sin"[29] and enjoyed already a certain divine grace. Original sin came to destroy that happy state. Scripture

---

23. According to Augustine, *De gestis Pelagii* 23.

[Saint Augustine, *On the Proceedings of Pelagius*, 23, ibid., 193.—Trans.]

24. *Epistula ad Demetriadem* 8, 17.

25. According to Augustine, *De gratia Christi* I, 27, 30: "ad operandum" "ad facilius operandum."

[Saint Augustine, *On the Grace of Christ*, 1.27, in *The Nicene and Post-Nicene Fathers*, ed. Schaff, trans. Holmes and Wallis, 228.—Trans.]

26. According to Tixeront, *Histoire des Dogmes dans l'antiquité chrétienne*, ch. XI.

27. Romans 7:25 [*sic*].

[The reference should read Rom. 7:24.—Trans.]

28. *De Genesi contra manichaeos* II, VIII, 32.

29. *De concept. et gratia* [*sic*], 33: "posse non peccare."

[The title of this work is actually *De correptione et gratia*, or in English, *On Rebuke and Grace.*—Trans.]

is strict on this point, and Saint Augustine himself relies on it.[30] Our nature is tainted, and without baptism, man is destined for damnation (according to John II, 54). Saint Augustine sees proof of this in the universal desolation of the world and in the misery of our condition, of which he paints a powerful picture.[31]

But these are the secondary effects of original sin. Others more intimate and more irremediable will indicate the extent of our misfortune. First, we have lost the freedom of the "ability not to sin."

We depend on divine grace. On the other hand, damnation is, in principle, universal. Humankind as a whole is doomed to the flames. Its only hope is divine mercy.[32] From this, there follows another consequence: the damnation of unbaptized children.[33]

Grace is then made more urgent. And we are dependent on this grace from three points of view: in order for us to preserve our tainted nature, in order to believe the truths of the supernatural order,[34] and in order to make us act according to those truths.[35] But this highest grace which is faith we do not merit by our works. However, we can merit, to a certain extent, that of beneficence.[36] In all cases, what determines our entire fate is Predestination. And Saint Augustine constantly returns to the gratuity of this doctrine.[37] The number of the chosen, just as that of the outcasts, is set once and for all and invariably. Only then does God consider our merits and demerits in order to determine the degree of our punishment. What we cannot know is the reason why this is so. Our freedom is a freedom to refuse the highest graces on the one hand, and to merit the secondary graces on the other. Our spontaneity applies only to the interior of divine omnipotence.[38]

---

30. Psalm 50; Job 19:4; Ephesians 2:3; above all Romans 5:12; John 3:5.

31. *Contra Iulianum* I, 50, 54, P.L. vol. 45, col. 1072; *De civitate Dei* XXII, 22; I, 3.

32. "Universa massa perditione." *De diversis quaestionibus ad simplicianum* I, *quaestione* II, 16.

33. *Contra Iulianum* III, 199, P.L. vol. 45, col. 1333.

[Camus mentions this teaching in a lecture he gave at the Dominican Monastery of Latour-Maubourg entitled "The Unbeliever and Christians," later published in *Resistance, Rebellion, and Death*, trans. Justin O'Brien (New York: Vintage Books, 1974), 72. The context is Camus' defense of himself against the charge of pessimism: "I was not the one to invent the misery of the human being or the terrifying formulas of divine malediction. I was not the one to shout *Nemo bonus* or the damnation of unbaptized children."—Trans.]

34. *De praedestione Sanctorum* 5, 7, 22.

35. *Epistulae* CCXVII.

36. *Epistulae* CLXXXVI.

37. *Enchiridion* XCVIII and XCIX. *Epistulae* CLXXXVI, 15. *De dono perseverantiae*, 17.

38. *De Gratia et libero arbitrio* 4.

2. The Word and the Flesh: The Trinity. We have grasped in reality what in Saint Augustine is specifically Christian. If we think back to Plotinian metaphysics, we will see the infinite distance that separates the two attitudes. Thus, at least we will not be misled by the frequent parallels between the two, and we will know to make allowances for Saint Augustine's Christianity in his Neoplatonism. As we have seen, what he has drawn from the Platonic authors is a certain conception of the Word. But his role was to include Christ in this conception and from there to develop it into the Word made flesh of the fourth Gospel. We must therefore follow closely to understand what Saint Augustine has been able to ask of Neoplatonism. We will then show how these borrowed conceptions were transformed by the doctrine of the Incarnation.

a) The Word: "[A soul of this kind (that is, a pure soul) will be where substance and reality and the divine are]—that is in god—there it will be with them and in him."[39] But Saint Augustine says: "The ideas are certain original and principal forms of things, i.e., reasons, fixed and unchangeable, which are not themselves formed and, being thus eternal and existing always in the same state, are contained in the Divine Intelligence."[40] He understands God through the heart, but also through intelligence. We see clearly that his conception is thus entirely philosophical, because the intelligible world that we marvel at reveals to us its secret. Our spirit, before the world, performs a double movement. Before the variety of beings produced by the intelligible, it distinguishes the idea that it encompasses, but its second effort synthesizes these ideas into a single reality that expresses them thus: "Then not only are they ideas, but they are themselves true because they are eternal and because they remain ever the same and unchangeable."[41]

---

39. Plotinus *Ennead* IV, III, 24: "C'est en Dieu, dit Plotin que l'âme pure habite avec les intelligibles."
[Plotinus *Ennead* 4.3.24, trans. A. H. Armstrong, Loeb Classical Library (Cambridge: Harvard University Press, 1984), 111.—Trans.]
40. *De diversis quaestionibus* LXXXIII, *quaestione* 46, no. 2, P.L. vol. 40, col. 30: "Les idées sont comme les formes premières ou les raisons des choses, stables et immuables, n'ayant point reçu leur forme éternelle par suite et toujours de même qui sont contenues dans l'intelligence divine."
[Saint Augustine, *On Various Questions,* 46, no. 2, in *The Fathers of the Church: Saint Augustine: Eighty-Three Different Questions,* ed. H. Dressler, trans. D. L. Mosher (Washington, DC: Catholic University of America Press, 1982), 80.—Trans.]
41. *De diversis quaestionibus* LXXXIII, *quaestione* 46, no. 2, P.L. vol. 40, col. 30: "Non solum sunt ideae sed ipsae verae sunt, quae eternae sunt, et ejus modi atque incommutabiles manent."
[Saint Augustine, *On Various Questions* 46, no. 2, ibid., 81.—Trans.]

"This reality," which Saint Augustine understands in this way as pure intelligence and the highest truth, "is God."[42] It is a Plotinian conception. What is at work here is the principle of participation. The ideas participate in everything divine. They are in it, and yet it is something more than them. We will reveal this relation better still through a vigorous text of *de Trinitate*:[43] "So because there is but one Word of God, *through which all things were made* (Jn. 1:1–6), which is unchanging truth, in which all things are primordially and unchangingly together, not only things that are in the whole of this creation, but things that have been and will be; but there is not a question of 'have been' and 'will be,' there they simply are; and all things there are life and all are one, and indeed there is there but one 'one' and one life."[44] The Plotinian method shows through here. But the moment Saint Augustine incorporates this doctrine of the Word Intelligence into the theory of the Trinity, things change their meanings. Plotinus actually arranges his hypostases in a hierarchy and affirms the distance that separates the One from Intelligence. Saint Augustine, in his account, started from God, not as the source of the other two essences, but as the only nature of the Trinity. "The one God is, of course, the Trinity, and as there is one God, so there is one creator."[45]

The three persons of the Trinity are therefore identical. From this there follow three fundamental consequences: the three persons have only one will and one operation. "They are supremely one without any difference of natures or of wills."[46] "It is therefore not the Word alone

42. "I think, therefore he is." If this has been compared to the cogito, it is also because the Augustinian God is an interior God.

43. In comparison to *Enneads* V, VII, 3; VI, VII, 3.

44. *De Trinitate* L, 4, G. I, no. 3. P.L. vol. 42, col. 888: "Puisque le Verbe de Dieu par qui tout a été fait est un; puisqu'il est la vérité immuable c'est en lui comme dans leur principe immuable que sont à la fois toutes choses: non seulement celles de ce monde présent, mais encore celles qui ont passé et celles qui viendront. En lui elles ne sont ni passées ni futures. Elles sont simplement et toutes sont vie et toutes sont un ou plutôt c'est une seule chose qui est, et une seule vie."

[Saint Augustine, *On the Trinity*, 4.1, no. 3, in *The Works of Saint Augustine*, vol. 5, ed. J. E. Rotelle, trans. E. Hill (Brooklyn: New City Press, 1991), 154.—Trans.]

45. *Contra Sermone* 3.

["Unis quippe deus est ipsa Trinitas et sic unus deus quomodo unus creator [*sic*]." This passage is actually from Saint Augustine *Contra sermonem Arianorum* 3.4. The text should read: "Unus quippe deus est ipsa Trinitas, et sic unus Deus, quomodo unus creator." Saint Augustine, *Contra Sermonem Arianorum*, in *The Works of Saint Augustine: A Translation for the 21st Century*, vol. 18, *Arianism and Other Heresies*, ed. John E. Rotelle, trans. Roland J. Teske (New York: New City Press, 1995), 142.—Trans.]

46. *Contra Maximinum* II, 10.

["Ubi nullam naturam esse, nulla est diversitas voluntatum (*sic*)." The full title of Augustine's text is *Contra Maximinum haereticum Arianorum Episcopum*. The passage

that has appeared on earth but the entire Trinity." "In the Incarnation of the Son it is the whole Trinity that is united to the human body."[47]

Each of the three persons is equal to the entire Trinity and to God himself, who contains the other two persons: "Therefore the Father alone or the Son alone or the Holy Spirit alone is as great as the Father and Son and Holy Spirit."[48] This theory of the Trinity attempts therefore to reconcile the equality and distinction of the Persons. This is a problem that already goes beyond Plotinianism but which makes use of its method. Moreover, Augustine connects his Christology to this doctrine of the Trinity, and it is thus that the Word is separated from Neoplatonic Intelligence.

b) The Flesh: The Word has already been made flesh, its body is real, earthly and born of a woman.[49] This union of body and word is indestructible. Man and Christ are one, and this is the whole Christian mystery: "The fact that the Word became flesh does not imply that the Word withdrew and was destroyed on being clothed with flesh, but rather that flesh, to avoid destruction, drew near to the Word . . . The same One who is Man is God, and the same one who is God is Man, not by a confusion of nature but by unity of person."[50] What one must note here is that the Word in Saint Augustine is increasingly Plotinian, and it is increasingly separated from Neoplatonism to the extent that the union of this Word and this flesh becomes more miraculous.

But everything is justified by one fact: Jesus' incarnation. Though the idea is contradictory, at least the fact is obvious. And moreover,

---

should read: "Ubi nulla naturarum, nulla est diversitas voluntatum." Saint Augustine, *Contra Maximinum haereticum Arianorum Episcopum*, in *The Works of Saint Augustine: A Translation for the 21st Century*, 18: 274.—Trans.]

47. *De Trinitate* II, 8, 9, P.L., vol. 42, col. 85.

[Although Camus' reference suggests that these quotations are taken from *De Trinitate*, they are actually a paraphrase from a passage from Tixeront's *Histoire des dogmes dans l'antiquité chrétienne*, 2:364–65: "Ce n'est pas le Verbe seul qui a apparu, mais toute la Trinité, mais Dieu . . . Dans l'Incarnation du Fils, l'acte qui a uni le Fils avec la nature humaine et qui l'a ainsi envoyé dans le monde est le fait de tout la Trinité.—Trans.]

48. *De Trinitate* VI, 9, P.L. vol. 42, col. 93: "Tantus est solus pater, vel solus Filius, vel solus spiritus Sanctus, quantus est simul Pater, Filius et Spiritus Sanctus."

[Saint Augustine, *On the Trinity* 6.9, in *The Works of Saint Augustine*, vol. 5, ed. Rotelle, trans. Hill, 211.—Trans.]

49. *Sermone* CXC, 2.

50. *Sermone* CLXXXVI, 1.

["Quod Verbum caro factum est, non Verbum in carnem pereundo cessit, sed caro ad Verbum ne ipsa perire, accessit . . . idem deus qui homo et qui deus, idem homo, non

considering the grandeur of the task, the grandeur of the miracle is understandable.

C. *Faith and Reason in Saint Augustine*

Admittedly it is not an exposition of Augustinian thought that we have claimed to offer, but just as well the task does not escape us. Regarding our subject, what was important was to examine a certain conjunction of two thoughts in our author, to attempt to define in them the living part and the acquired part, and to draw from them conclusions that concern the relation between Neoplatonism and Christianity. This is why we have centered our study of Augustinianism around the two particularly suggestive themes for this subject. It remains for us only to draw the conclusions from this particular study. By so doing, we will have the opportunity to recount the general features that, up to now, we have examined in detail. And by placing ourselves on the inside of Christian metaphysics at this point in its evolution, we will be able to envision the latter and to see how all its effort ends, with the assistance of Saint Augustine, with the reconciliation of a metaphysics and a religion, of the Word and the Flesh, without, to tell the truth, Christianity's original physiognomy being lost in that reconciliation.

Let us summarize here only the significance of Augustinianism in relation to this evolution. "But in all the regions where I thread my way, seeking your guidance, only in you do I find a safe haven for my mind, a gathering-place for my scattered parts, where no portion of me can depart from you. And sometimes you allow me to experience a feeling quite unlike my normal state, an inward sense of delight which, if it were to reach perfection in me, would be something not encountered in this life, though what it is I cannot tell."[51] Saint Augustine arrives at the point where Plotinian conversion comes to an end. It is the same goal that

confusione naturarum, sed unitate personae [*sic*]." The Latin text should read: "Quod Verbum caro factum est, non Verbum in carnem pereundo cessit; sed caro ad Verbum, ne ipsa periret, accessit . . . Idem deus qui homo et qui Deus, idem homo; non confusione naturae, sed unitate personae."

[Saint Augustine, *Sermons on the Liturgical Seasons*, trans. Sister Mary Sarah Muldowney (New York: Fathers of the Church, Inc., 1959), sermon 186.1, p. 10.—Trans.]

51. *Confessions* L. X, chap. XL: "Dans aucune de ces choses que je parcours à votre lumière, je ne trouve un lieu de repos pour mon âme, si ce n'est en Vous; en Vous ma dispersion se recueille et de vous plus rien de mieux n'échappe. Et quelquefois vous me

both of them seek, but their paths, though crossing occasionally, are nevertheless different. Augustinianism declares at each step the inadequacy of philosophy. The only intelligent reason is the one that is enlightened by faith. "True philosophy begins by an act of adherence to the supernatural order which will liberate the will from the flesh through grace, and thought from scepticism through revelation."[52] One could not emphasize this point too much.

The dialogue between Faith and Reason is placed, for the first time, in full view by Saint Augustine: this was the whole history of Christian evolution. One often wants Christian thought to be something superfluously added to Hellenic doctrine. The claim is true. Faith has ended by accepting the Reason of which it knew nothing. But if we believe Saint Augustine, this was in order to give it a very remarkable standing.

"If thou hast not understood, said I, believe. For understanding is the reward of faith. Therefore do not seek to understand in order to believe, but believe that thou mayest understand."[53] This reason is dulled. It is clarified by the light of Faith. There are two things in Augustinian faith: the adherence of the spirit to supernatural truths and the humble abandonment of man to the grace of Christ. One must believe, not *that* God exists, but *in* God.

"But you will probably ask to be given a plausible reason why, in being taught, you must begin with faith and not rather with reason."[54] Reason must be humbled: "The beatitudes begin with humility. 'Blessed are the poor in spirit,' that is to say, those not puffed-up, while the soul submits itself to divine authority."[55]

---

faites entrer dans un état intérieur très extraordinaire, et goûter je ne sais quelle douceur, qui si elle se consomme en moi sera je ne sais quoi qui ne sera pas la vie présente."

[Saint Augustine, *Confessions*, 10.40, trans. R. S. Pine-Coffin (Baltimore: Penguin Books, 1961), 249.—Trans.]

52. Étienne Gilson, conclusion to *Introduction à l'Étude de Saint Augustin*.

53. In *Joannis Evangelicum*, tractatus 29, 6, P.L. vol. 35, col. 1630: "Si non potes intelligere, crede ut intelligas, praecedit fides, sequitur intellectus. Ergo noli quaerere intelligere ut credam, sed crede ut intelligas."

[Saint Augustine, *Homilies on the Gospel of John*, 29.6, vol. 7, p. 184. The first sentence of this quotation is not, as Camus indicates, from *Homilies on the Gospel of John*, but from *Sermon* 118.1.—Trans.]

54. ["Quam tibi persuadetur non prius ratione quam fide te esse docendum (*sic*)." Camus offers no reference for this text. It is from Saint Augustine *De Utilitate Credendi ad Honoratum*. The Latin text should read: "Qua tibi persuadeatur non prius ratione quam fide te esse docendum." Saint Augustine, *On The Usefulness of Believing*, in *Library of Christian Classics*, vol. 6, *Augustine: The Early Writings*, trans. John H. Burleigh (London: SCM Press, 1953), 308.—Trans.]

55. *De sermone domini in mente* I, chap. III, no. 10, P.L. vol. 34, col. 1233: "La béatitude

Thus we can grasp that the Alexandrian Word had served Christian thought without harming it. By understanding Saint Augustine, we can understand the entire course of Christianity's evolution: to soften progressively Greek reason and to incorporate it into its own edifice, but in a sphere in which it is inoffensive. Beyond this sphere, it is obliged to yield its authority. In this regard, Neoplatonism provides Saint Augustine with a doctrine of humility and of faith. This was its role in the evolution of Christianity: to assist this relaxing of Reason, to lead Socratic logic into religious speculation, and in this way to pass on this ready-made tool to the Fathers of the Christian church.

In this sense, it is possible to consider Augustinianism as a second revelation, the revelation of a Christian metaphysic that follows the initial revelation of Evangelical faith. The miracle is that the two may not be contradictory.

II. Christian Thought at the Threshold of the Middle Ages

Here ends the evolution of primitive Christianity and begins the history of Christian doctrine.

Augustinianism marks both an end and a beginning. We have indicated by what path evangelical thought has reached this point. The principal fact in its evolution is its break with Judaism and its entrance into the Greco-Roman world.[56] From that moment on, the fusion begins. Prepared by Oriental religions, Mediterranean thought is inclined to be impregnated by this new civilization. Though Neoplatonism can be considered as the artisan of this fertilization, it is true that it too is born of this Greco-Oriental syncretism. The dogmatic formulas of Christianity are products of a combination of this syncretism and Evangelical faith's

---

commence par l'humilité. Bienheureux les pauvres en esprit c'est-à-dire ceux qui ne s'enflent pas, mais qui se soumettent à l'autorité divine."

[Saint Augustine, *Our Lord's Sermon on the Mount* 1.3, no. 10, in *The Nicene and Post-Nicene Fathers*, ed. P. Schaff, trans. W. Findlay (Grand Rapids: Wm. B. Eerdmans, 1956), 6.—Trans.]

56. [Camus repeats this account of Christianity's break with Judaism and entrance into the Greco-Roman world in his essay "The New Mediterranean Culture": "In the beginning Christianity was an inspiring doctrine, but a closed one, essentially Judaic, incapable of concessions, harsh, exclusive, and admirable. From its encounter with the Mediterranean, a new doctrine emerged: Catholicism." In *Lyrical and Critical Essays*, 192.—Trans.]

own givens. Announced by Paul and John, elaborated by the Greeks, converted to Christianity, these formulas find their fullest expression in Augustinianism, but not, however, before a group of Christians had been lost in false reconciliations.

At bottom, the enigma is that this fusion had worked at all, because though the Greco-Roman world's sensibility was open to the Gospel, Reason itself refused to accept a certain number of postulates. Providentialism, creationism, philosophy of history, a taste for humility, all the themes that we have pointed out run counter to the Greek attitude. This Greek naïveté of which Schiller speaks was too full of innocence and light to abdicate without resistance. The task of the conciliators was to transform the very instrument of this attitude, that is to say, Reason, governed by the principle of contradiction, into a notion shaped by the idea of participation. Neoplatonism was the unconscious artisan of this reconciliation. But there is a limit to the flexibility of intelligence. And Greek civilization, in the person of Plotinus, stopped halfway. It is in this gap that it may be possible to sense precisely Christianity's originality. Of course, it is the Alexandrian Word that Christian thought has transported into its dogmas. But this Word is not distinguished from God himself, and it is generated and not emanated.

But the Word is in direct contact with its creature, for whom it came to die. And that which would appear contradictory to a Greek spirit is justified in the eyes of Christians by one fact: Jesus' appearance on Earth and his incarnation. This is the word we find at the beginning and the end of the evolution of Christian metaphysics. It is also proof that Christianity has given up none of its primitive flavor in order to veil itself in Greek thought.

On the eve of the Middle Ages, the ancient human theme of the journey of a God on the earth is applied, for the first time, to the metaphysical notion of divinity. And the more the metaphysic is developed, the greater will be the originality of Christianity, insofar as it will increase the distance between the Son and Man and the notions that it transfigures.

Conclusion

We have bound ourselves to the solution of two problems: the one, extremely vast, touching the relations between Christianity and Hellenism, the other, itself implicit in the former. The second problem deals with the role of Neoplatonism in the evolution of Christian thought. The material was too vast to have hoped to provide definitive responses. But we have examined, on the one hand, three stages in the evolution of Christian thought, and on the other hand, the culmination of the work of Greek thought in Neoplatonism. A simple comparison has furnished us with a few conclusions.

Christianity has borrowed from Greek thought its material and from Neoplatonism a method. It has maintained intact its profound truth by treating all difficulties on the level of the Incarnation. And if Christianity did not exactly originate this disconcerting way of posing problems, without a doubt Greece had absorbed it. Herein Greece had seen other problems. This, at least, remains precise, but how many other difficulties remain: the role played by Philo in the formation of Alexandrian metaphysics, the contribution of Origen and Clement of Alexandria to dogmatic Christianity, and the numerous influences we have evaluated: Kabbala, Avesta, Indian philosophies, or Egyptian Theurgy. But the exposition suffices. Let us hold ourselves to a few observations. Many speak of the hellenization of early Christianity. And as far as morality is concerned, the claim is no doubt true.[1] But Christian morality is not the

---

1. The first systematic treatise on Christian morality, that of Ambrose, in the second half of the fourth century, is based, not on the Gospel, but on the *De Officiis* of Cicero.

object of education; it is an inner asceticism that amounts to accepting faith. On the contrary, according to our work, one must speak rather of the christianization of a decadent Hellenism. And here the words have a historical and even a geographical meaning.

But finally, is it possible, at the end of this study, to determine what constitutes the novelty of Christianity? Are there even notions that are properly Christian? The question is certainly topical. In fact, it is a particular paradox of the human spirit to grasp the facts and to be unable to comprehend the synthesis: for example, an epistemological paradox of a science, certain in its facts, but in that case insufficient, or satisfactory in its theories, but thus uncertain; or a psychological paradox of a self, perceptible in its parts, but inaccessible in its profound unity. In this regard, history does not deliver us from our anxieties, and to return to the profound novelty of the Gospel seems like an impossible task. We see well beneath these influences the syncretism from which Christian thought is born. But we are also aware that, were it dismantled entirely into foreign elements, we would still recognize it as original because of a more subdued resonance than the world has yet heard.

And if we reflect on the principal themes of Christianity—Incarnation, Philosophy according to history, the misery and sorrow of the human condition—we recognize that what matters here is the substitution of a "Christian man" for a "Greek man." This difference, which we manage to define poorly in the doctrines, we experience by comparing Saint Jerome of the desert to those stricken with temptation and the young who listened to Socrates.[2] Because if, moreover, we believe Nietzsche, and if we agree that the Greece of darkness that we mentioned at the outset of this work, the pessimistic Greece, deaf and tragic, was the mark of a strong civilization, it is necessary to admit that Christianity in this regard is a

---

2. And *Epistulae* XXII, 7: "Moi, oui moi, qui par crainte de la géhenne m'étais condamné à une telle prison, habitée seulement par les scorpions et les bêtes sauvages, souvent je me croyais transporté au milieu des danses virginales, j'étais pâle de jeûnes et mon imagination bouillonnait de désirs." Accoding to P. de Labriolle, *Histoire de la littérature latine chrétienne*, 451.

[Saint Jerome, *Letter to Eustochium*, 22.7: "There was I, therefore, who from fear of hell had condemned myself to such a prison, with only scorpions and wild beasts as companions. Yet I was often surrounded by dancing girls. My face was pale from fasting, and my mind was hot with desire [in a body cold as ice]." In *Ancient Christian Writers: The Letters of St. Jerome*, No. 33, ed. J. Quasten and W. J. Burqhardt, trans. C. C. Mierow (New York: Newman Press, 1963), 140.—Trans.]

rebirth in relation to Socraticism and its serenity.[3] "Men," says Pascal, "being unable to cure death, are wise not to think about it."[4] The whole effort of Christianity is to oppose itself to this slowness of heart. From this is defined the Christian man and, at the same time, a civilization. Ch. Guignebert in his *Christianisme antique* speaks of Christian thought as a religion "of fanatics, the hopeless, and the beggars."[5] The statement is true, but not as the author would like it.

Be that as it may, at the time of Saint Augustine's death, Christianity was formed into a philosophy. It is now sufficiently armed to resist the tempest in which all will founder. During the long years, it remains the only common hope and the only effective shield against the calamity of the Western world. Christian thought had conquered through its universality.

3. [Camus here repeats Nietzsche's argument in *The Birth of Tragedy*. According to that argument, Christianity renews in some measure the tragic universe of the ancient Greeks. "It was this semblance of 'Greek cheerfulness' which so aroused the profound and formidable natures of the first four centuries of Christianity: this womanish flight from seriousness and terror, this craven satisfaction with easy enjoyment, seemed to them not only contemptible, but a specifically anti-Christian sentiment." Friedrich Nietzsche, *The Birth of Tragedy*, trans. Walter Kaufmann (New York: Vintage Books, 1967), 78. Camus also repeats Nietzsche's charge that ancient tragedy died at the hands of Socrates' rationalism. Ibid., 95–96. The question of Christianity's seriousness in relation to the world of the ancient Greeks was one to which Camus later returned in *The Rebel*. For a discussion of his various answers to that question, see Ronald D. Srigley, "Eric Voegelin's Camus: The Limitations of Greek Myth in *The Rebel*," paper presented at the meeting of the Eric Voegelin Society, the American Political Science Association Meeting, Philadelphia, 2003.—Trans.]

4. [Camus offers no reference for this quotation.—Trans.]

5. [Again Camus offers no reference.—Trans.]

Epilogue

Camus and Christianity:
The *Diplôme d'études supérieures* of 1936

⎯⎯⎯⎯⎯⎯⎯⎯⎯⎯⎯⎯⎯⎯⎯⎯⎯ ⇒‡‡

How did Camus see Christianity? One can find almost everywhere in his work many elements of a reply to this question. I will consider here only one text, but which has the value of a seed, a thesis of which the title indicates the approach: *Christian Metaphysics and Neoplatonism*. It is a youthful text, written in 1936 when Camus was not yet twenty-three years old. It was compulsory: a Master's thesis (*Diplôme d'études supérieures*), the writing of which was necessary to qualify for the competitive exam of the *agrégation*. Camus did not take that exam due to health reasons. The text remained unpublished until its inclusion in the Pléiade Edition of Camus' work, of which it occupies close to eighty pages.[1]

I cannot help reading Camus' thesis with the eye, and the red pen, of the professor I was. A professional habit for which I will perhaps be forgiven. The scholarship is very often second hand, but Camus indicates it honestly each time he cites a given commentator. His bibliography is incomplete, even for the languages he read, including of course his maternal French. In this respect, it is strange that Camus seems not to have known a book that explores his subject, that of the Dominican scholar André-Jean Festugière, *The Religious Ideal of the Greeks and the Gospels* (1932).

---

1. I use the page numbers of this Edition of the text.

In any case, the book, coming from an author who has yet to mature, is of good quality, and I would have liked to have had the opportunity to read Master's theses of this level more often . . .

§ The Importance of Gnosis

The book's center of gravity is the comparison of two figures who give expression to thoughts Camus opposes and treats chronologically: the Neoplatonism of Plotinus (Chapter 3: Mystic Reason) and the "Christian metaphysics" of Saint Augustine (Chapter 4: The Word and the Flesh).

The Introduction demonstrates the existence, alongside the Hellenic light, of a "Greece of darkness" (1000) that Nietzsche had already seen (1076). A Greece of religious aspirations, a Greece of mysteries, and later on the Hellenized Mediterranean, invaded by cults from the Middle East. It is this mysticism that Plotinus had attempted to capture and formulate in the terms of Greek philosophical thought.

However, the most interesting parts of the book, at least in my opinion, are the first two chapters, which deal with "Evangelical Christianity" and "Gnosticism" respectively, the latter being a blanket-term for a combination of doctrines apparent in the second and third centuries of our era and which shared a common denial of the world's value.

Camus demonstrates a real interest in Gnostic thinkers that is well informed. Of course, he did not know the Coptic library of Nag Hammadi, which was discovered in 1945 and which has transformed our knowledge of Gnosticism. Camus assumes his place among authors who have given Gnosticism philosophical respectability, whatever their attitude toward it may have been: neutral historical studies (Hans Jonas), slightly obsessive critique (Eric Voegelin), downright questionable flirting (Jacob Taubes), or frank adherence (Harold Bloom). About one gnostic, Marcion, Camus writes: "In this pessimistic view of the world and this proud refusal to accept, we find the echo of a completely modern sensibility" (1029). This slightly awkward sentence anticipates the ideas of the "absurd" and "revolt" ("refusal [. . .] to accept") that Camus will place at the center of his own thought.

It is obviously not a question of attributing to Camus the entire wild mythology constructed by those authors whose doctrines he summarizes. However, one can find in a certain gnostic sensibility the anticipation of themes that were dear to Camus, and I am not the first person to note it. Hence *The Stranger*, which could very well be the title of a gnostic treatise. This is in fact the case with one of the Nag Hammadi texts, the *Apocalypse of Allogenes*.[2] And in chapter 2 of *The Rebel*, Camus will mention again, in cursory fashion, the gnostic solution to the problem of evil.

§ Christianity?

One may well wonder what precisely Camus has in mind when he speaks of Christianity. The categories by means of which he attempts to understand it are numerous and deserve a thorough examination, which I can only outline here.

Camus understood Christianity as a "civilization," an idea he poses on three occasions in the Introduction to his thesis and which he repeats later on (1018–1019). Camus, who was at the time still a member of the Communist Party, expresses himself in the same way as the self-proclaimed defenders of "Christian civilization," who were, by the way, not always very Christian in their methods. Camus also speaks in his title and on occasion in the body of the text of a "Christian metaphysic," employing the language of certain neo-Thomists. He does not hesitate to speak of Saint Augustine as a "second revelation" (1004, 1040, 1062, 1073). Elsewhere, he speaks of Christianity as an "attitude toward the world," an attitude he describes throughout the book as pessimistic in the customary rather than philosophical sense of this term. If none of these categories seems to me entirely wrong, none is perfectly adequate either. But all are derived, at bottom, from the word "Christianity" itself. The suffix "ity" suggest in effect either a system of thought, as in Platonism, or a style of life, as in Judaism.[3]

The fact remains that the word "Christianity" would scarcely have any meaning without Christ himself, and it is he who, in Camus' thesis, is paradoxically conspicuously absent.

---

2. *The Nag Hammadi Library in English*, 3rd Edition, ed. James M. Robinson (San Francisco: Harper, 1988), 491–500.

3. Brague's meaning is clearer in French, in which Christianity is *christianisme*, and for which the suffix would therefore be an "ism" (translator's note).

§ A Fact

I would risk the following hypothesis: perhaps Camus could only see Christianity precisely because it was Christianity he sought to see, whereas Christianity itself is not interested in Christianity, but in Christ. Camus set out in search of what is "distinctively Christian" (1069). However, Augustine, whom Camus turned into a metaphysician, had replied: "What is Christian in Christianity is Christ." Nevertheless, I find in Camus' text passages that perhaps reveal he had at least an inkling of this insight, the insight that at the center of the whole affair is a *fact*.

Thus, in the first chapter we read: "Here, it is not a matter of reasoning, but of a fact: Jesus is come. To Greek wisdom, which is only a science, Christianity opposes itself as a state of affairs" (1012). And in the conclusion: "what would have seemed contradictory to a Greek mind is justified in the eyes of Christians by a fact: the appearance of Christ on earth and his incarnation" (1075).

But a fact must be addressed as it wishes to be addressed, otherwise one misses it. One has here moreover an entirely Greek thought: Aristotle requires that one tailor one's approach to the object one seeks to address.[4] It is the object that determines the faculty that will prove adequate to match it; it is not the faculty that will decide what is entitled to appear to it.

We can take one step more and ask ourselves how this rule applies when the fact is a person. A personal object is addressed in a particular perspective, neutral in relation to the various faculties. What is personal speaks to our affectivity (whether I love it or detest it), but also to the understanding (what does it say exactly?) and to the moral sense (is it good? Should I imitate it?)

§ A Person

The fundamental Christian fact, the height of which not only all emotional experiences but also all concepts strive to reach, is a person. Jesus is a man who behaves very unusually. He performs miraculous healings, but this was also said of the Emperor Vespasian and Apollonius of

4. Aristotle, *Nicomachean Ethics*, I, 3, (1094b23–1095a15).

Tyana.[5] However, other characteristics are without parallel, unique, unprecedented, and caused a slightly scandalized astonishment among his contemporaries: he speaks with authority, without laying claim to a Master's teaching, as did the rabbis (Matthew 7: 29). He forgives sins, which only God can do (Mark 2: 7). In prayer, he dares to call God, not "Father," but *abba*, which is the Aramaic equivalent of "daddy" (Mark 14: 36).

Now, if the content of the revelation is a person, one understands better the Christian themes that, according to Camus, run counter to what he called the "Greek attitude," namely, "providentialism, creationism, philosophy of history, and a taste for humility" (1074).

The fundamental concept here is what Camus calls, perhaps not very skillfully, the "philosophy of history" (1010, 1036). This concept calls forth the three ideas of an absolute beginning (Creation), of a glance that captures the entire course of human history (providence), and of an existence that we do not owe to ourselves (humility). Now, this conception of the becoming of humanity and even of the universe is a generalization of the history that constitutes the life of each person (his biography) with its characteristics: birth, uniqueness, linearity, irreversibility, the accumulation of the past that snowballs over the present, and the freedom to choose at each moment which direction to go.

It is also the personal nature of what is revealed that allows us to overcome certain alternatives. For Evangelical Christianity, writes Camus, "It is not a matter of knowing and understanding, but of loving" (1003). The alternative is a faulty one. What would that knowledge be, when held by someone, which would be emotionally neutral? It could not be about a person as such, but a state of things. When it is concerned with a person, which is inevitably the case, love is a way to knowledge. Equally, the object of love must remain accessible to knowledge. Because what would a love be that did not allow its object the independence it needs in order not to be absorbed, swallowed up?

It is the same with the oversimplified oppositions by which Camus attempts to comprehend the differences between what is Greek and what is Christian, between a self-sufficient man and a dependent one. A person, without losing any of his freedom, is what he is through his

---

5. See Philstratus, *The Life of Apollonius of Tyana*, Vol. 2, ed. F.C. Conybeare (Cambridge: Harvard University Press, 1912).

"role" (in Latin, *persona*) in an exchange with others, which permits him rather to become what he is. In short, Camus is reasonably well informed about Christianity understood as "Christian metaphysics," which he ascribes to it. But perhaps he strangely neglected to pause a little longer over the person from which the adjective "Christian" derives its meaning.

By Rémi Brague
Translated by Ron Srigley

Bibliography

Auxiliary Works to Christianity

Loisy.—*Les Mystères païens et le mystère chrétien.* Paris, 1919.
Cumont.—*Les Religions orientales dans le paganisme romain.* 1907.
Cumont.—*Les Mystères de Mithra.*
Foucart.—*Recherches sur l'origine et la nature des mystères d'Éleusis.* 1895.
Foucart.—*Les Associations religieuses chez les Grecs.*
Gernet & Boulanger.—*Le Génie grec dans la Religion.* Paris, 1932.

Alexandrian Metaphysics

(a) Texts

Plotin.—*Ennéades I to VI,* 5 inclusive, Bréhier translation; VI, 5 to VI, 9, Bouillet translation.
Porphyre.—*Vie de Plotin.* Volume I of Bréhier's translation.
Proclus.—*Commentaires du Parménide.* Chaignet translation. 3 volumes.
Damasius.—*Des principes.* Chaignet translation. 1898.

(b) Studies

Vacherot.—*Histoire critique de l'école d'Alexandrie.* 3 volumes. 1846–1851.

Simon.—*Histoire de l'école d'Alexandrie.* 2 volumes. Paris, 1844, 1845.

Ravaisson.—*Essai sur la métaphysique d'Aristote.*

Bois.—*Essai sur les origines de la philosophie judéo-alexandrine.* Toulouse, 1890.

Bret.—*Essai historique et critique sur l'école juive d'Alexandrie.*

Bréhier.—*Les Idées philosophiques religieuses de Philon d'Alexandrie.* Paris, 1908.

Kurppe.—*Philon el la Patristique* in "Essais d'histoire": Philosophie. Paris, 1902.

Bréhier.—*La Philosophie de Plotin.* Paris, 1903.

Arnou.—*Le Désir de Dieu dans la philosophie de Plotin.* Paris, 1921.

Guyot.—*L'Infinité divine depuis Philon le Juif jusqu'à Plotin.* Paris, 1908.

Picavet.—*Hypostases plotiniennes et Trinité chrétienne.*

Annuaire de l'École des Hautes-Études, 1917.

Guitton.—*Le Temps et Éternité chez Plotin et Saint Augustin.* Paris, 1933.

Picavet.—*Plotin et les Mystéres d'Éleusis.* Paris, 1903.

Cochez.—*Les Religions de l'Empire dans la philosophie de Plotin.* 1913.

Cochez.—*Plotin et les Mystéres d'Isis.* "Revue néoscolastique," 1911.

C. Elsee.—*Neoplatonism in Relation to Christianity.* Cambridge, 1908.

Inge.—*The Philosophy of Plotinus.* London, 1918.

Lindsay.—*The Philosophy of Plotinus.* 1902.

Fuller.—*The Problem of Evil in Plotinus.* Cambridge, 1912.

Caird.—*The Evolution of Theology in the Greek Philosophers.* 2 volumes. Glasgow, 1904.

Plotinus: II, pp. 210–346.

Gnosticism

(a) Studies

De Faye.—*Introduction à l'étude du Gnosticisme.* Paris, 1903.

——*Gnostiques et Gnosticisme.* Paris, 1913.

——*Clément d'Alexandrie.* 2nd edition. Paris, 1898.

Matter.—*Histoire critique du Gnosticisme.* 2 volumes. 2nd edition. Paris, 1844.

Mansel.—*The Gnostic Heresies.*

King.—*The Gnostics.*

Salmon.—*Gnosticisme.*

Amelineau.—*Essai sur le Gnosticisme égyptien.* Guimet, XIV.

De Beausobre.—*Histoire du Manichéisme.* 2 volumes. 1739–1744.

Cumont.—*Recherches sur le Manichéisme.* Volume I: *la Cosmogonie manichéenne d'après Théodore Bar. Khoni.* Brussels, 1908.

Alfaric.—*Les Écritures manichéennes.*

(b) Texts

Cf. above all:

Tertullian.—*De praescriptionibus adversus Haeresos.* In *Patrologie latine de Migne,* volume II, columns 10 to 72.

——*Adversus Marcionem.* In *Patrologie latine de Migne,* volume II, columns 239 to 468.

——*Adversus Valentianum.* In *Patrologie latine de Migne,* volume II, columns 523 to 524.

The Evolution of Christianity

General Works

Tixeront.—*Histoire des Dogmes dans l'antiquité chrétienne.* 3 volumes. Paris, 1915, 1919, 1921.

P. de Labriolle.—*Histoire de la littérature latine chrétienne.* Paris, 1920. 2nd edition, 1923.

Puech.—*Histoire de la littérature grecque chrétienne depuis les origines jusqu'à la fin du IVe siècle.* 3 volumes. Paris, 1928–1930.

Puech.—*Les Apologistes grecs du IIe siècle de notre ère.* Paris, 1912.

Le Breton.—*Les Origines du dogme de la Trinité: des origines au concile de Nicée.* 1919. 2nd edition, 1923.

Hellenism and Christianity

(a) Studies

Havet.—*Le Christianisme et ses origines.* 4 volumes. Paris, 1800–1884.

Aubié.—*Les Chrétiens de l'Empire romain de la fin des Antonins au début du IIIe siècle.* Paris, 1881.

Boissier.—*La Fin du paganisme.* 4th edition. 1903.

Corbiere.—*Le Christianisme et la fin de la philosophie antique.* Paris, 1921.

Toussaint.—*L'Hellénisme et l'Apôtre Paul.*

Lenain De Tillemont.—*Mémoires pour servir à l'Histoire ecclésiastique des six premiers siècles.* 1702.

Dourif.—*Du Stoïcisme et Du Christianisme . . . .* Paris, 1863.

Bréhier. "Hellénisme et Christianisme aux premiers siècles de notre ère." *Revue philosophique.* 27-5-35.

T. R. Glover.—*The Influence of Christ in the Ancient World.*

(b) Polemics

P. de Labriolle.—*La Réaction païenne.* Paris, 1934.

Aubié.—*La Polémique païenne à la fin du IIe siècle.* Paris, 1878.

Rougier.—*Celse ou le conflit de la civilisation antique et du christianisme primitif.* Paris, 1925, and a translation of Celsus's *Discours vrai.*

Paul Allard.—*Julien l'Apostat.* 3 volumes. Paris, 1900–1903.

——*Julien l'Apostat, oeuvres.* Bridez edition. Paris, 1932.

(c) On Saint Augustine

See the reasoned and more or less complete bibliography in Gilson: *Introduction à l'Étude de Saint Augustin.* Paris, 1931.

I. Works.—Migne: *Patrologie latine.* Volumes XXII to XL inclusive.

Principal works cited in this work:

(a) *Confessions.* Volume XXXII, columns 659 to 905.

De civitate Dei. Volume XXXVIII, columns 13 to 806.

Soliloques. Volume XXXVII, columns 863 to 902.

Méditations. Volume XXXVII, columns 901 to 944.

De beata vita. Volume XXXII, columns 959 to 977.

(b) Against the Heresies:

De duabus animis contra Manichaeos. Volume XXXIX, columns 93 to 112.

Contra Fortunatum manichoeum. Volume XXXIX, columns 111 to 130.

Contra Adimandum manichoei discipulum. Volume XXXIX, columns 129 to 174.

De Natura Boni contra manichaeos. Volume XLII, columns 551 to 578.

Contra Iulianum. Volume XLIV, columns 1094 to 1612.

De Natura et gratia. Volume XLI, columns 199 to 248.

De Gestis Pelagii. Volume XLI, columns 319 to 360.

De gratia Christi et peccato originali. Volume XLI, columns 359 to 416.

De gratia et libero arbitrio. Volume XLI, columns 881 to 914.

(c) *Epistolae.* Volume XXXIII.

(d) *Sermones.* Volume XXXVI.

General Studies

E. Gilson.—*Introduction à l'étude de saint Augustin.* Paris, 1931.

Portalié.—"Article saint Augustine." In *Dictionnaire de Théologie catholique.* Volume L, columns 2268 to 2472. 1902.

Nourrisson.—*La Philosophie de saint Augustin.* 2 volumes. 2nd edition. 1809.

Alfaric.—*L'Évolution intellectuelle de saint Augustin.* Volume I: *Du Manichéisme au Néoplatonisme.* 1918.

Boyer.—*L'Idée de vérité dans la philosophie de saint Augustin.* Paris, 1920.

Boyer.—*Christianisme et Néoplatonisme dans la formation de saint Augustin.* Paris, 1920.

Martin.—*Saint Augustin.* 1901.

Grandgeorge.—*Saint Augustin et le Néoplatonisme.* 1896.

Cayre.—*La Contemplation augustinienne.* Paris, 1927.

The Notion of Christian Philosophy

E. Gilson. "La Notion de philosophie chrétienne." *Bulletin de la Société française de philosophie.* March 1931.

E. Bréhier. "Le Problème de la philosophie chrétienne." *Revue de métaphysique et de morale.* April 1931.

Souriau. "Y a-t-il une philosophie chrétienne?" *Revue de métaphysique et de moral.* July 1932.

E. Gilson.—*L'Esprit de la philosophie médiévale.* 2 volumes. Paris, 1932. Chap. I: "Le Problème de la philosophie chrétienne."

Index